Science, models and toys
Stage 3

A Unit for teachers

Published for the Schools Council by
Macdonald Educational, London and New York

©Schools Council Publications 1974

First impression 1974
Second impression (with amendments) 1976

ISBN 0 356 04351 7

Published by
Macdonald Educational
Holywell House
Worship Street
London EC2

850 Seventh Avenue
New York 10019

All rights reserved. No part of this publication may be reproduced, stored in a retrieval system, or transmitted, in any form or by any means, electronic, mechanical, photocopying, recording or otherwise, without prior permission of the publishers.

The chief author of this book is:

Don Radford

The other members of the Science 5/13 team are:

Len Ennever	Project Director
Albert James	Deputy Project Director
Wynne Harlen	Evaluator
Sheila Parker	
Roy Richards	
Mary Horn	

Made and printed by Waterlow (Dunstable) Ltd

General preface

'Science 5/13' is a project sponsored jointly by the Schools Council, the Nuffield Foundation and the Scottish Education Department, and based at the University of Bristol School of Education. It aims at helping teachers to help children between the ages of five and thirteen years to learn science through first-hand experience using a variety of methods.

The Project produces books that comprise Units dealing with subject areas in which children are likely to conduct investigations. Some of these Units are supported by books of background information. The Units are linked by objectives that the Project team hopes children will attain through their work. The aims of the Project are explained in a general guide for teachers called *With objectives in mind* which contains the Project's guide to Objectives for children learning science, reprinted at the back of each Unit.

Acknowledgements

The Project is deeply grateful to its many friends: to the local education authorities who have helped us work in their areas, to those of their staff who, acting as area representatives, have borne the heavy brunt of administering our trials, and to the teachers, heads and wardens who have been generous without stint in working with their children on our materials. The books we have written drew substance from the work they did for us, and it was through their critical appraisal that our materials reached their present form. For guidance, we had our sponsors, our Consultative Committee and, for support in all our working, the University of Bristol. To all of them we acknowledge our many debts; their help has been invaluable.

Metrication

This has given us a great deal to think about. We have been given much good advice by well-informed friends, and we have consulted many reports by learned bodies. Following the advice and the reports whenever possible we have expressed quantities in metric units with Imperial units afterwards in square brackets if it seemed useful to state them so.

There are, however, some cases to which the recommendations are difficult to apply. For instance we have difficulty with units such as miles per hour (which has statutory force in this country) and with Imperial units that are still in current use for common commodities and, as far as we know, liable to remain so for some time. In these cases we have tried to use our common sense and, in order to make statements that are both accurate and helpful to teachers we have quoted Imperial measures followed by the appropriate metric equivalents in square brackets if it seemed sensible to give them.

Where we have quoted statements made by children, or given illustrations that are children's work, we have left unaltered the units in which the children worked—in any case some of these units were arbitrary.

Contents

1	**1**	**Introduction**
1	1.1	Why Stage 3?
1	1.2	What can be got out of toys?
2	1.3	How can the Unit be used?
2	1.4	For whom is this book intended?
3	1.5	What do we mean by group-working?
4	1.6	How are groups formed?
4	1.7	Starting the work
4	1.7.1	Group-working
8	1.8	Records children make
8	1.9	Discussion in the classroom
8	1.10	**Work-cards/sheets**
9	1.10.1	Hints on preparing work-cards
10	1.11	Integration
10	1.12	Sources of information
11	**2**	**Boats**
11	2.1	The use of plastics guttering
12	2.2	What force is required to move a boat through the water?
14	2.3	Wakes and waves
15	2.4	Testing a streamlined hull
16	2.5	Follow-up
17	2.6	Motors
17	2.7	Elastic motors
17	2.7.1	Investigations with the motor
18	2.7.2	Investigations into the properties of rubber
19	2.8	Electric motors
19	2.9	Diesel or glowplug engines
19	2.10	Steam engines
21	2.11	Clockwork motors
21	2.12	Flotation
22	2.13	Sources of materials

24	**3**	**Balls**
24	3.1	Stage 1, 2 and 3 work
25	3.2	Energy and the mechanics of bouncing
25	3.2.1	Sample work-sheet: energy and bouncing balls
28	3.2.2	Summary
28	3.3	The connection between the height of drop and the height of bounce
28	3.4	Rolling balls down slopes
30	**4**	**Ballista—mangonel**
31	4.1	Measurements: length—accuracy and approximation—an outline of a possible class discussion
31	4.2	The range of the mangonel
34	4.3	Altering the range of the mangonel
34	4.4	Energy
36	**5**	**Cameras**
36	5.1	What can we do using photographic materials?
36	5.1.1	Light-sensitive materials
37	5.1.2	Photo-silk-screen printing in a school
38	5.1.3	Blueprint material
39	5.1.4	Gelatine/dichromate
39	5.1.5	Colour dyes
39	5.1.6	Blueprint paper used in a camera
39	5.1.7	Photograms, photographs without a camera
42	5.2	Making a pinhole camera
45	5.3	Working with a pinhole camera
46	5.4	Developing and printing
47	5.5	Simple equipment and materials
47	5.5.1	For developing a film (black and white)
47	5.5.2	For printing a film
48	5.5.3	Sources of information—black and white photography
48	5.5.4	Sources of information—colour photography
48	5.6	Use of a camera for recording
49	5.7	Useful apparatus for school use
49	5.8	Postscript
51	**6**	**Electrical toys**
51	6.1	Low-voltage toys and safety
51	6.2	Electricity and safety
52	6.3	How do we start and what do we do?
52	6.4	The use of electrical toys
52	6.5	Notes on apparatus, toys and methods employed
52	6.5.1	Shunting wagons
54	6.5.2	Simple timing unit
57	6.5.3	Making a simple dc electric motor
58	6.5.4	Example of a branching programme for fault-finding
59	6.6	Radio control of models
59	6.7	Sources of supply

Page	Section	Title
60	**7**	**Trains and cars**
60	7.1	Gears
62	7.2	Gears and a car
64	7.3	Other gears in everyday life
64	7.4	Engineless cars
64	7.4.1	Ideas which might develop
65	7.4.2	A problem of hills and speeds
67	7.4.3	Switchback
67	7.4.4	Looping the loop
67	7.4.5	Problems of weight
68	7.5	Electro Rockets
68	7.5.1	Some investigations
68	7.5.2	Energy storage devices
69	**8**	**Flying models**
70	8.1	Hot-air balloons
70	8.1.1	Steps in the construction of a hot-air balloon
72	8.1.2	Flying hot-air balloons
72	8.1.3	Working with a hot-air balloon
74	8.1.4	Development work
74	8.2	Paper aeroplanes
76	8.2.1	Making paper aeroplanes
77	8.2.2	Ideas to follow up
77	8.3	Gliders
78	8.3.1	Three simple balsa models
81	8.3.2	Solid balsa wood chuck glider
82	8.4	Flying models
84	**9**	**Objectives**
84	9.1	Attitudes, interest and aesthetic awareness
84	9.2	Observing, exploring and ordering observations
85	9.3	Developing basic concepts and logical thinking
85	9.4	Posing questions and devising experiments or investigations to answer them
85	9.5	Acquiring knowledge and learning skills
86	9.6	Communicating
86	9.7	Appreciating patterns and relationships
86	9.8	Interpreting findings critically
87	9.9	The Unit and Objectives
88	**10**	**Apparatus and materials**
91		**Objectives for children learning science**
99		**Index**

'A new scientific truth does not triumph by convincing its opponents and making them see the light, but rather because its opponents eventually die, and a new generation grows up that is familiar with it.'

Max Planck, *Scientific Autobiography and Other Papers*

'For, to speak once for all, man only plays when in the full meaning of the word he is a man, and he is only completely a man when he plays.'

Friedrich von Schiller, *Aesthetical Letters and Essays*

1 Introduction

1.1 Why Stage 3?

It is not intended to produce a Unit with a subject-theme running through it, but rather to put together a number of snippets, each of which indicates work that can be undertaken in the top forms of junior schools, in middle schools or in secondary schools by children who have reached Stage 3.*

Some of the toys chosen are dealt with in the Unit *Science from toys Stages 1 and 2*, therefore the work suggested here follows on as a natural development.

The use of a topic which is limited and fairly complete in itself, while not fitting into a continuous pattern in the way that a structured O-level investigation does, might provide painless opportunities for pupils undergoing the metamorphosis from primary to secondary education. Topics based on toys might seem to be associated with primary schools, but the work could be tackled with the resources and know-how of the secondary school using primary school methods. It is suggested that work of this type affords chances:

a. To bridge the gap between the primary and the secondary ways of teaching.

b. For teachers to assess the potentials of pupils before starting formal work.

c. For pupils to acquire some of the basic skills required of them.

d. For teachers who are not used to them to try less formal methods.

e. For pupils to grow used to the more structured demands of the secondary school in respect of time-tabling, methods of working, homework, changes of teachers and rooms, and the whole life of the school, by carrying out work which, while largely controlled by themselves, fits the new framework.

1.2 What can be got out of toys?

Although secondary schools are much concerned with the acquisition of knowledge usually, in an orderly pattern, the development of attitudes and interests are equally important. Indeed, in these days when scientific and technical knowledge is doubling every ten years or so, one is faced with the impossible task of training a pupil for a job which does not at present exist but will be based on future discoveries. The development of attitudes of mind and behaviour are thought by some to be of greater importance than factual learning. This is not to say that knowledge is unimportant, but only that perhaps we need to look harder at our educational objectives. The Science 5/13 Project has constructed a list which is discussed fully in the Project's publication *With objectives in mind.*

The table of toys shows the areas of knowledge which could be profitably explored either by using the toys themselves or by using the interest generated by the toys. As mentioned in *Science from toys Stages 1 and 2,* the toys children play with are often only starting-

*A full discussion of what is meant by Stage 3 is given in With objectives in mind. *Briefly, it refers to a stage in mental development when a child is in the transition between thinking with the aid of concrete operations and thinking involving abstractions.*

Toy	Ideas which could arise
Boats* (Chapter 2)	Air flow, streamlining, forces, velocity, stability, relationship—force and velocity, balancing forces, variables, terminal velocity, testing propulsion systems, mechanical systems, energy, possible links with history, geography and handicraft.
Balls* (Chapter 3)	Materials, simple measurements, influence of chance on measurements, simple energy conversions, trajectories—gravitational force, colliding balls—simple ideas on momentum, variables.
Ballista mangonel* (Chapter 4)	Variables, chance trajectories, energy.
Cameras (Chapter 5)	Light, pinhole camera, light-sensitive materials, chemicals, solutions, techniques used, lens, colours, resolving power of lens, photograms and a method of illustrating dislocations in metals
Electrical toys (Chapter 6)	Motors, circuits, cells, magnetism, mechanical systems, energy.
Trains, cars, Hot Wheels, Rockets* (Chapter 7)	Energy, mechanical systems, friction, slopes, speed, motion in a circle.
Things which fly: model aircraft (Chapter 8)	Forces, gliders, engines, links with handicraft.
Engines: steam, diesel/glowplug	Fuels, air and gases, energy, work, horsepower, graphs, links with handicraft.

points for investigations. They provide motivation because they are familiar to children and children work flexibly with them, but the initial start requires a grown-up's help. Some teachers have commented that investigations have started only as the result of a carefully contrived situation during which they have asked suitable leading questions. So it is important that teachers should be prepared and know the potentialities of a particular toy.

In summary, it could be said that toys either provide starting-points for work or could be used as part of an investigation. The work which results might help a child to acquire knowledge, and it could help him to attain some desirable objective.

1.3 How can the Unit be used?

It has been suggested that a topic on toys, using *Science from toys Stages 1 and 2* and this Unit, could be used to introduce science to children newly come to a secondary school.

The Unit could also be used during more formal work to illustrate a particular point. In this respect, the previous section does suggest some of the ideas which could arise by working with a particular toy.

On the other hand a theme such as 'Energy'† could be introduced by the use of toys, and by careful selection a number of useful experiences could be acquired by children for drawing on later.

1.4 For whom is this book intended?

This is a book for teachers. It is not intended for pupils until the language and ideas have been suitably translated to suit their needs.

Also dealt with in Science from toys *but only at Stages 1 and 2.*

†*Energy is also the main theme of* Change Stage 3.

The Unit contains ideas and requires methods of thinking which are suitable only for pupils who have reached a certain level of development. In his article 'How to assess science courses', Michael Shayler gives a diagram showing the percentage of children at any age established in various stages of development. He suggests that by the age of thirteen only ten percent of the child population is in Piaget's Formal Operation Stage. In other words, only ten percent are capable of making extensive use of abstract thinking.*

The Unit is for pupils who are approaching Piaget's Formal Operation Stage, not for those who are still in the Concrete Operation Stage. (For explanations of these terms, please turn to page 92.)

The Unit deals with energy and suggests ways of approaching this topic through the group-working methods used in primary schools. Chapter 1 is concerned with ways of working in the classroom and presents ways and means of organising this type of work. It also outlines the function of the teacher and gives one interpretation of the teaching/learning process.

However, this is essentially a practical book presenting tried ideas and suggesting answers to classroom problems.*

1.5 What do we mean by group-working?

The term 'group-working' means different things to different people. To one teacher it means everyone doing the same experiment but working in groups. To

---

*See With objectives in mind, page 47.

*See With objectives in mind, pages 50-54.

another teacher it means groups of children carrying out different and often unrelated work at the same time and then pooling the results of their investigations. There is a great deal of difference between the two meanings in the working of individuals, and in the basic philosophy behind the work.

We are not attempting to prescribe *one* method of working, but to indicate what has been seen to be successful in the trial schools. During the trials, when schools were visited and the opinions of teachers canvassed, it became apparent that increased formality in teaching methods and organisation leads to ease of timing and timetabling, to ease of testing and to the teachers making sure that everyone had covered the syllabus. At the same time, there was a lack of child involvement other than in a passive state. On the other hand, while there are considerable administrative difficulties, group-working coupled with subject integration leads to more intellectual flexibility and the ability for children to carry on with a piece of work untrammelled by the timetable. It also involves children in the planning of their work, which leads to greater motivation than if the children were only passive receptors.

1.6 How are groups formed?

What are the criteria for the formation of groups? They can be formed upon:

a. A friendship or social basis.

b. A purely random method, for example, alphabetical arrangement.

c. An ability grouping, for example, bright children grouped with bright or a group spanning the ability range.

Reasoned arguments can be presented for and against any of the arrangements, but generally the one which seems to be most successful is the grouping based upon friendship. It is child-based and generally is one in which there is a fairly homogeneous or compatible pattern of ability, and likes and dislikes.

1.7 Starting the work

Another starting problem is, 'How do I introduce the topic?' Usually this has been done by holding a class discussion and getting children to bring things to school. Once both the teacher and the class can handle an object or look at an exhibition, there is often an interchange of ideas which can be skilfully used to reveal a problem. If one group is prepared to tackle a certain aspect of a problem other groups might care to look at the problem in a different way, historically for example, and so the field of investigations is widened.

Group-working enables a class to cover a wider field than if each individual had to do all the work himself. It also provides a *raison d'être* for groups to present reports on their work to the rest of the form. A pupil then has a reason for making records; he also has something authoritative to say.

1.7.1 Group-working
a. Groups and topics from the children's viewpoint:

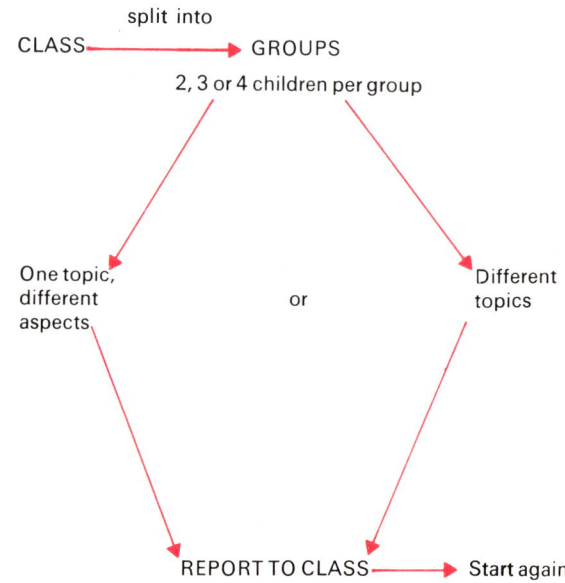

b. **Groups and topics from the teacher's viewpoint (O-level Nuffield approach):**

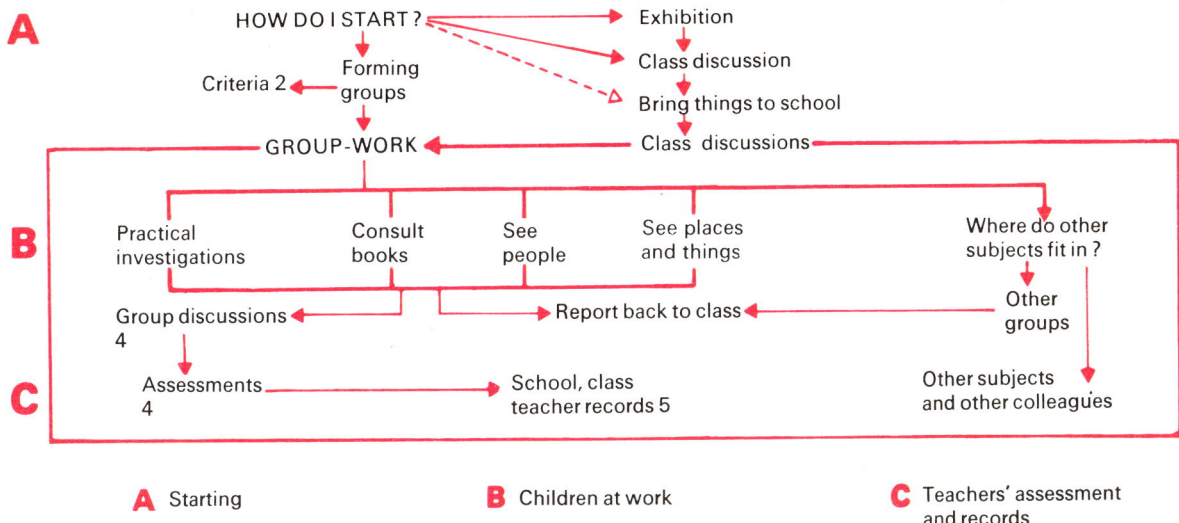

A Starting   **B** Children at work   **C** Teachers' assessment and records

Decisions have to be made on:

1. What topic(s) is (are) suitable?

2. How should the groups be selected?

3. Shall one topic be taken and different aspects of it investigated or shall different topics be taken?

4. How are the pupils getting on? What help do they require?

5. What records does the teacher have to make? How can the teacher make his or her assessments?

(Key: the numbering of the above questions corresponds to the numbers in chart *b* (above) showing the teacher's viewpoint of groups and topics.)

When starting fresh work, there is one very important factor which ought to be considered. Are the children ready for the work? This means asking two supplementary questions:

a. Have the children developed sufficient mental skill to carry out abstract reasoning?* In other words, have they reached what we call Stage 3? For an explanation of Stage 3, see page 92.

b. Have the children had appropriate experiences on which to base the work?

If the answer to either question is no, then it would be more profitable to start with *Science from toys Stages 1 and 2*. The brighter child will most likely be able to progress rapidly to *Science, models and toys Stage 3* once he has come to terms with the new ideas. On the other hand, a number of pupils will need to stay with *Science from toys Stages 1 and 2* for some time until they have developed sufficiently. Even bright pupils who lack knowledge and practical experience benefit from Stages 1 and 2 work, and an attempt to go to Stage 3 without adequate preparation is not too productive. This was borne out by some work carried out in a college of education where students were asked to work with a Stage 3 Unit without first working with the companion Stages 1 and 2 volume. They found the work hard going unless they looked at the earlier Unit or they had previous experience on which to base their ideas and work.

*See With objectives in mind, *pages 46–48*.

Diagram 1 Planning the work in the classroom

For work on change the following pattern might be useful.

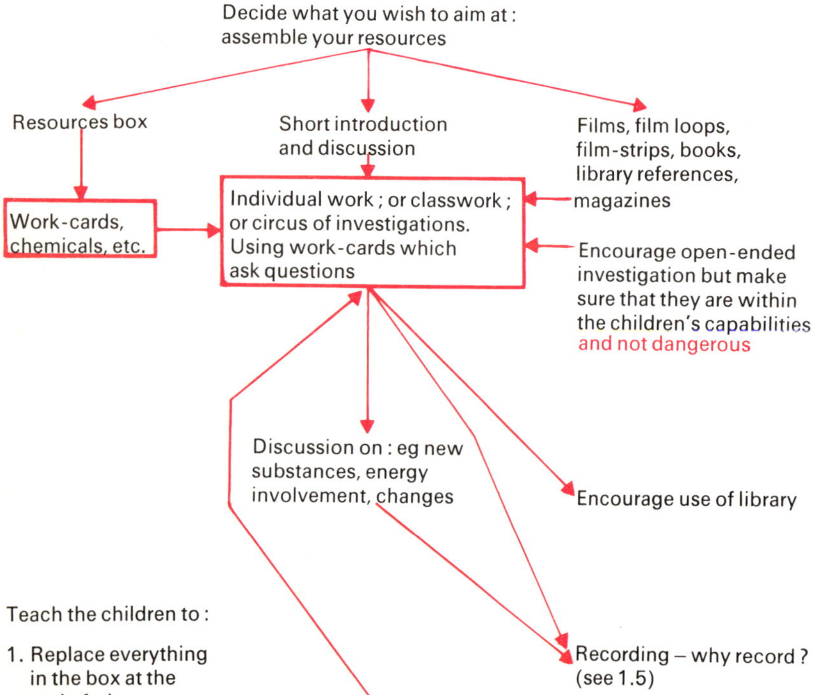

Decide what you wish to aim at: assemble your resources

- Resources box
  - Work-cards, chemicals, etc.
- Short introduction and discussion
- Individual work; or classwork; or circus of investigations. Using work-cards which ask questions
- Films, film loops, film-strips, books, library references, magazines
- Encourage open-ended investigation but make sure that they are within the children's capabilities **and not dangerous**

Discussion on: eg new substances, energy involvement, changes

Encourage use of library

Recording — why record? (see 1.5)

Teach the children to:

1. Replace everything in the box at the end of a lesson

2. Replenish from store stocks of materials when below a stated amount, eg a line or a bottle

   or

   hand in a note stating that material *X* needs topping up

3. Read instructions carefully and to *come to you if they do not understand anything they are told to do*

If some interesting by-ways are opened up, follow them but don't get lost. Discussions may suggest further practical investigations and these are valuable to keep interest alive and make the children feel that they are involved and that they are tackling their problems. The art is in structuring a situation so that children want to find out what you want them to find out! They will doubtless also find out much that you had not expected

Diagram 2

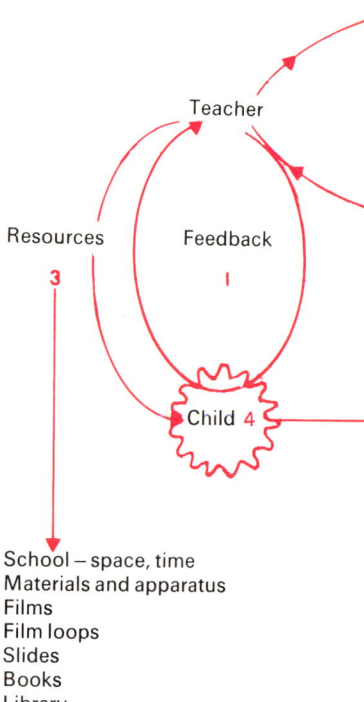

Teacher

Resources   Feedback

3

Child **4**

School — space, time
Materials and apparatus
Films
Film loops
Slides
Books
Library

1, **2**, **3** represents the teaching process, ∿**4** the interface where teacher and pup[il] interact, and **5** the acts of receiving the information, and processing it in such a w[ay] that the individual can use it some time i[n the] future. This leads to ideas, concepts, generalisations, which a child can use at various levels. The information must be digested *a* if it is to be usefully employed not swallowed in large chunks — which w[ill] lead to mental indigestion and an inabilit[y to] use what is learned

The learning/teaching process

Diagram 3 How a teacher helps a child to learn

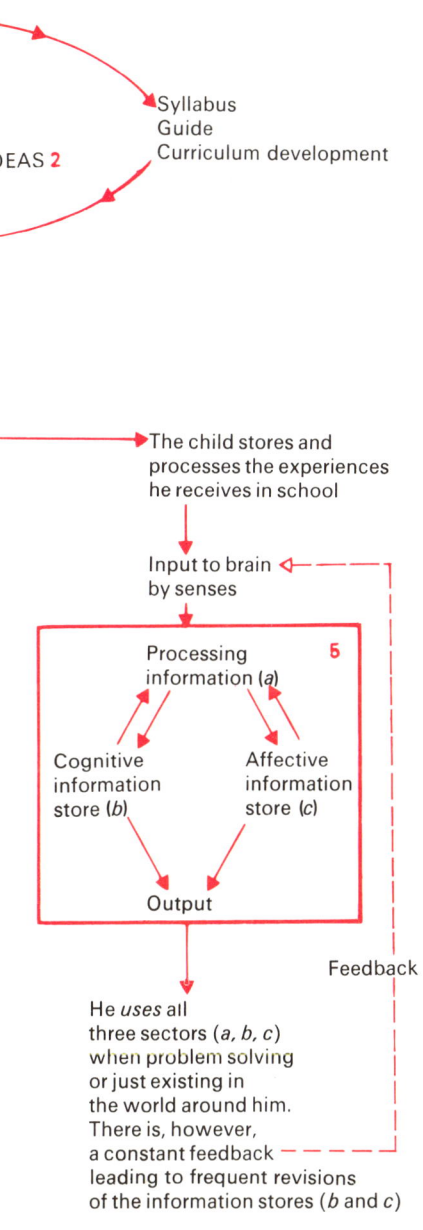

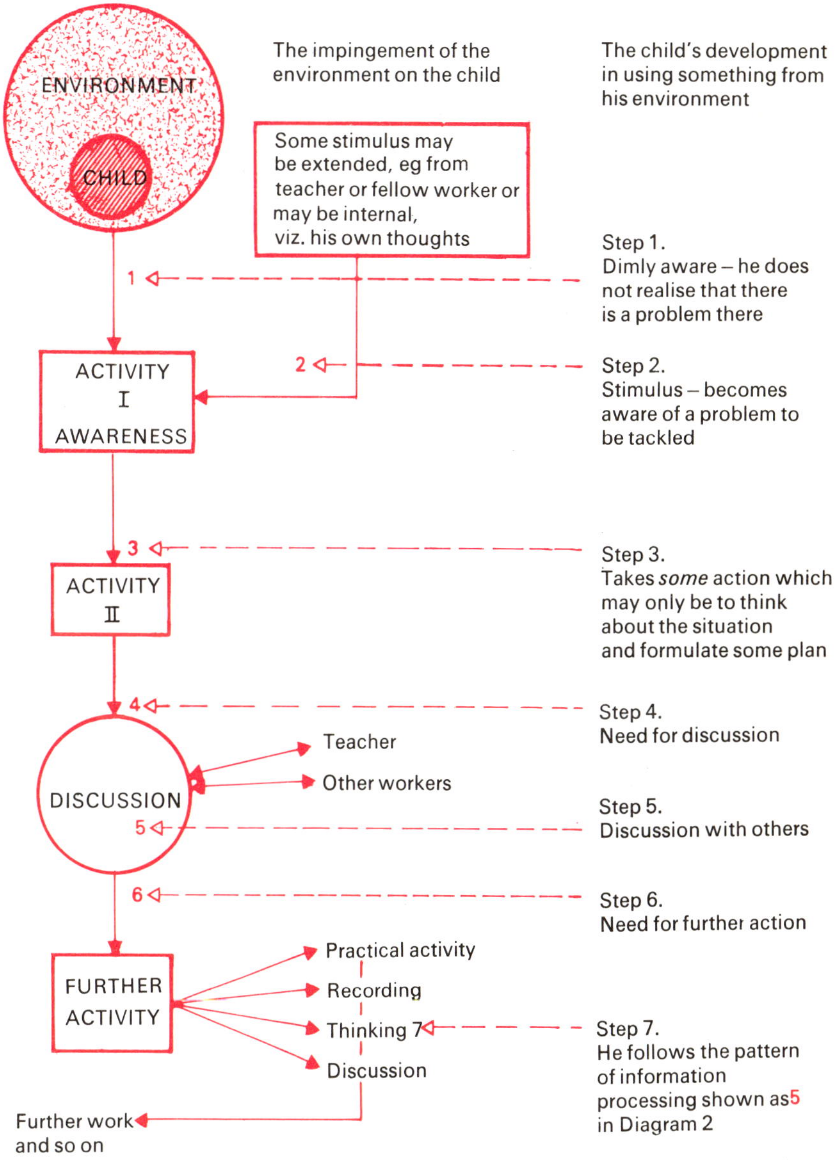

1.8 Records children make

The recording of observations needs to be encouraged and the teacher can suggest ways which are appropriate both for the children and the material being recorded. It is not always necessary for everything to be recorded in writing; there is no reason why a tape recorder cannot be used if it is available. Teachers are being urged to conduct examinations in 'as nearly as possible the same medium of expression as that in which the pupil or student will eventually make use of his attainment' (*Examinations Bulletin*, DES pamphlet no. 84, HMSO, (1964), page 12.)*

Many children will make far more use of the spoken than the written word when they leave school. To marshal facts and present arguments clearly are just as difficult to a speaker as to a writer. The main difference is that the speaker is relieved of the mechanical chore of writing; however, he might be well advised to marshal his facts in *note* form before he starts to speak. Many children are inhibited from making written records because they lack the manual dexterity and spelling skills needed of a writer. On the other hand, such children could be encouraged to make spoken records illustrated by photographs, drawings, graphs and collages. A simple electric circuit involving a battery and an electromagnet was effectively represented by a child who constructed a collage using a wrapper from a battery, string to represent the wire and a nail with string wound round it for the electromagnet on an electric bell.

In general, children's records are of two kinds:

a. The personal record for his own use some time in the future.

b. A suitable record to explain to other people what he has been doing.

---

*In a later Bulletin, (1965), *page 49: 'We should be concerned that a pupil can use the spoken word to demonstrate his understanding.'*

1.9 Discussion in the classroom

Discussion can be carried out at two levels:

a. In groups, when points which are relevant to the problem in hand can be considered.

b. Class discussion, during which matter of more general interest or importance can be talked about.

Children far more readily accept a regulation (eg a safety regulation), a convention (eg name and form at the top of all papers handed in), or a method of working (handling test-tubes and burners) if they can talk about it and perhaps be led to adopt it as the result of discussing ways of tackling a problem. All this takes time, but it is time well spent if as a result children acquire a natural way of working which can speed up their work in later classes.

When children investigate problems, skilfully maintained discussion can initiate a host of ventures and help to sustain them through difficult periods by digging deeper and throwing up interesting ideas. In this respect, the teacher is the catalyst.

1.10 Work-cards/sheets

The decision whether to use work-cards or not must be left to individual teachers.† Cards have the advantage that a teacher can attend to other children while the work-card group is carrying on with its investigations, and there is no reason why a work-card cannot pose some open-ended questions and not be just a 'cookbook'. The main disadvantage is that work-cards are liable to induce a state of stasis, for once they are produced the author becomes disinclined, after having spent so much time and energy on compiling them, to alter them. Another serious disadvantage is that they take a long time to prepare. This criticism can be met if teachers work together and thrash out basic ideas and each undertakes to produce a section, the final work-card being a collection of the work produced by the group of teachers.

A work-card/sheet used in conjunction with a cassette tape recorder is often very useful for slow readers. Such a tape can give not only instructions for the practical work but can also say:

'Go to cupboard 3, on shelf . . . you will find . . . . Look at the photograph in the file . . . . Read page . . . . Go to the library . . . . Now switch off . . . .

1.10.1 Hints on preparing work-cards
1. Decide the scope and extent of the card, and at whom the card is aimed.

2. Do not try to cover too much material on one card.

3. Prepare a rough of the materials you wish to cover. Separate out: instructions, questions, results and conclusions.

4. Break instructions down into separate sentences each giving one command.

5. Consider whether the instructions could be given in the form of a flow chart. This is of particular use when complicated instructions are given involving several operations that have to be carried out at the same time (see flow chart on right).

---

†*Bibliography:*
1. Bosworth, D. P., 'Teaching science individually through programmes', School Science Review, *vol. 48, no. 166,* (1967), *pages 702–9.*
2. Kamm, M. D., 'Teaching a basic science course to mixed ability group', School Science Review, *vol. 51,* (1969), *pages 633–4.*
3. Hamilton, D. F., 'Nuffield science in unstreamed classes in a comprehenisve school', Forum, *vol. 10, no. 3,* (1968), *pages 100–1.*
4. 'Nuffield 'O' Level Sciences: sources or courses?', School Science Review, *vol. 50, no. 173,* (1969), *pages 263–9.*
5. Reid, D. J., and Booth, P., 'The use of individual learning with the Nuffield Biology Course', School Science Review, *vol. 50, no. 173,* (1969), *pages 493–506.*
6. Townsend, Ian J., 'Science for the special child, Parts 1 & 2', School Science Review, *vol. 53, no. 184,* (1972), *pages 175–96.*

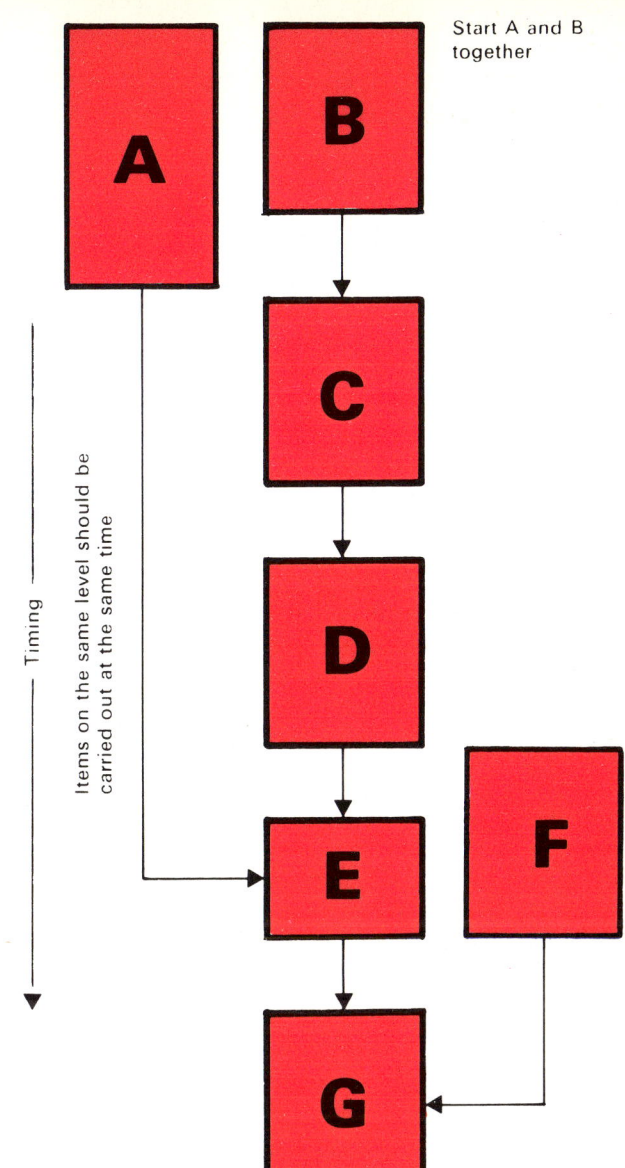

6. Decide what photographs/magazine illustrations would be useful and have the greatest impact, eg photographs involving personalities and places known to pupils.

7. Questions fall into two categories: those intended to promote some physical act or discovery and those which help pupils reach some conclusion by logical deduction. Try to link logic questions to produce a conclusion.

8. When using a series of questions, make sure that the steps between successive questions are not too great for your pupils. With an unstreamed class, be prepared for some questions not to be answered.

9. Make the work-card visually attractive. See if the art department can offer any advice, eg the use of capitals, lower-case or a mixture; spacing; use of coloured paper on which to type or write the instructions, for example:

Red—Instructions.
Blue—Questions.
Yellow—Results/observations.
Green—Conclusions or script containing spaces which have to be filled in so making a summary.

Standardise these colours so that in a collection the colour-coding is uniform.

Decide upon the size and material of the card.

10. Provide a working paste-up and try it out. Then alter it in the light of experience and produce two final editions; cover one with transparent plastic film and file the other.

1.11 Integration

Education in primary schools is not so fragmented as it is in secondary schools. Pupils have to accept and adapt to this abrupt change from one system to the other in a very short time. Experiments are being made in some secondary schools to group subjects and time in the first two years, so that one teacher takes a class for a substantial part of the week using a flexible timetable that does not prescribe exactly when a subject should be taken. The teacher is responsible for several subjects which are timetabled together. Thus he may take science, mathematics and geography, or science, history and English, or any other combination depending on his inclinations and abilities.

It often seems that a teacher who is able to cover a range of subjects in the junior forms of a secondary school is of more use in helping to achieve an integrated system than one who is specialised in only one subject of the curriculum.

Another way in which integration could take place is for teachers of different subjects to work out some scheme to cover their common subject areas.* Although this sounds desirable, such ideas are largely Utopian, and cooperation is the exception rather than the rule. There are some schools which are working along these lines; they are helped by the school's layout, which encourages cooperation due to the absence of specialist rooms and the provision of working spaces within the class area.

1.12 Sources of information

Often a reference is made to a particular book. Possibly this is not to hand or is not in the school library.

Try:

Local library; ask the local library to obtain the book through the Libraries Lending Scheme.

Teachers' Centre.

The local branch of the Association for Science Education.

Local college of education, college of further education, university.

*See With objectives in mind, *pages 5–8, 49, 54.*

2 Boats

The study of boats has proved very popular among children (see *Science from toys Stages 1 and 2*). They can investigate stability and shapes, methods of propulsion and how to test one boat against another using a length of plastics guttering as a testing tank. All these activities can be studied to a greater depth with increased sophistication and with more resources. As an example of this study, the following suggestions are given.

2.1 The use of plastics guttering

This component can be used in a study of the shapes of hulls. The basic set-up is shown in the diagram below left.

With the apparatus shown on the left the boat moves along the same distance as the weight falls. The simple pulley system, shown below right, can double the horizontal distance travelled for the same height of fall.

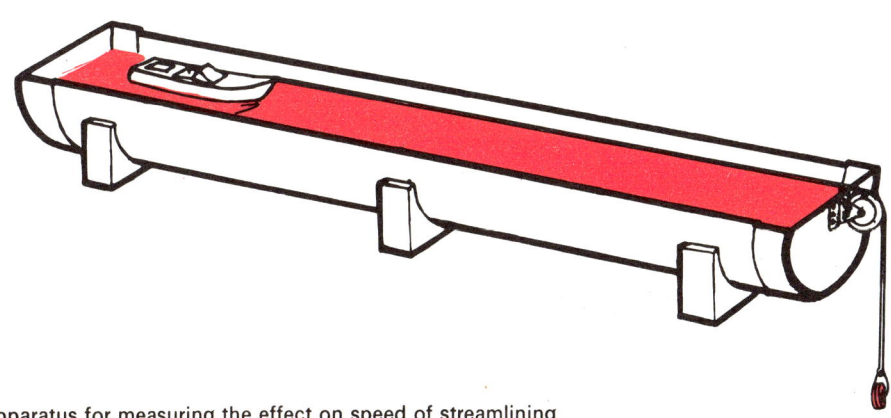

Apparatus for measuring the effect on speed of streamlining

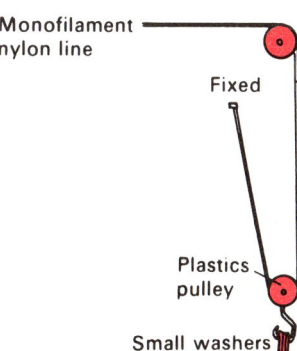

In place of the plastics pulley, a bent paper clip can be used

11

Pulley systems using Meccano:

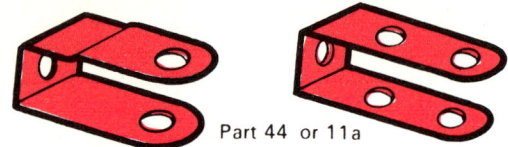

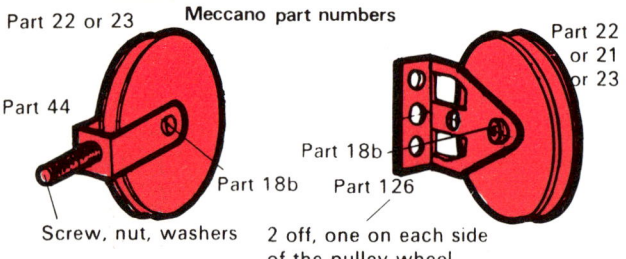

Meccano pulleys for the apparatus.

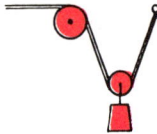

A pulley system.

Devise a pulley system to provide for an even longer length of guttering.

2.2 What force is required to move a boat through the water?

A start could be made by using a bought toy boat and towing it through the water using different forces (using washers as weights). The following problems arise:

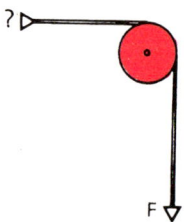

a. Use of a pulley system. If the force downwards is F, what is the horizontal force? Can we measure it? How? What units should we use for measuring it?

b. How can we measure the speed of the boat?

c. At the beginning the boat accelerates. Shouldn't we measure the speed when it has reached top speed for that particular force? Where else do we come across 'terminal velocities'? (See *Structures and forces Stage 3*.)

d. Does it matter if the towing line rests on the water? Or should it be kept out of the water at all times?

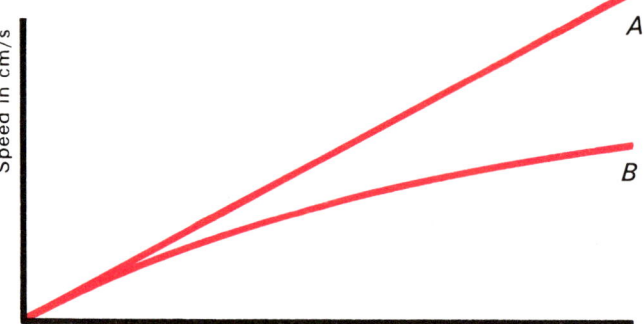

e. How does the speed vary with the force applied? Is there a linear relationship (*A*) or is it more complicated (*B*)? (For low speeds—low Reynold's number—there seems to be a square law relationship, namely, doubling the speed or halving the time requires four times the force.)

f. How can the results be expressed most conveniently and attractively?

g. Suppose we are measuring the time it takes a boat to cover a set distance and it comes to ten seconds; then we measure how long it takes for the towing line itself to cover the same distance and it comes to one and a half seconds. Should we make allowance for this 'line drag', and if so, how?

h. What happens if a detergent is added to the water? Does the quantity of detergent influence the effect?

i. Try sea water instead of tap water. (Artificial sea water: three percent common salt solution.)

j. Can a more complicated pulley system be devised so that the length of guttering can be increased?

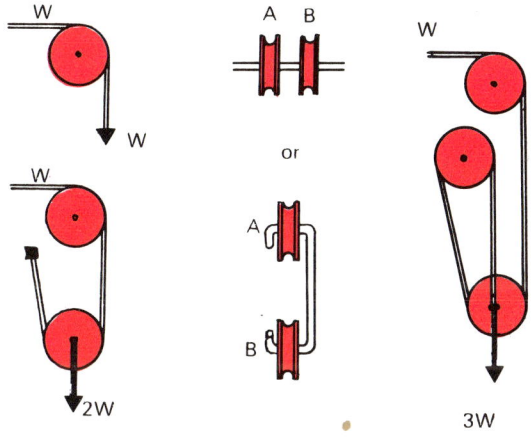

k. Can an inclined plane system be used to increase the 'length of pull'? Can a toy truck running down a slope be used? How can we measure the horizontal pulling force?

l. By now children should realise that when making measurements there is no 'right' result; there is a spread of readings. What is the spread of readings in measuring length, force and time? (See sections 4.1, 4.2.) How do the spreads influence the final result? Can we ignore some variations? When must we not ignore the variations? How accurately can we measure our length, force and time? If we keep the length and force constant during our investigation, do we always get the same time if we use the same boat? Is there a spread of results? What should we do about this?

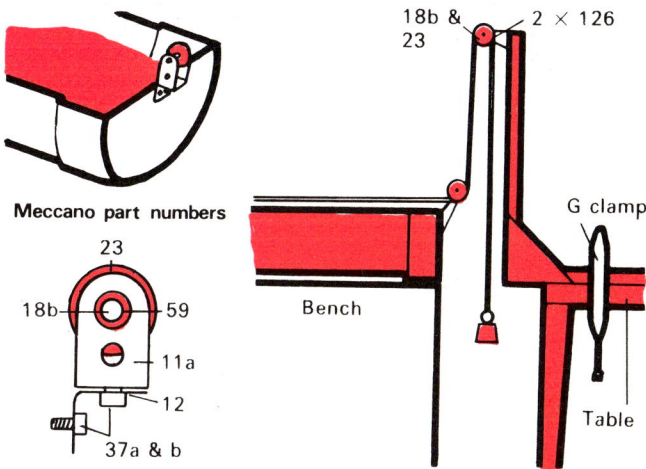

Obtaining a longer drop by using fixed position pulleys

m. If an electric boat is available, measure the pulling force it can exert while remaining stationary with the motor on.* This force is called its static thrust. Next measure its speed and compare this with the speed it attains when it is towed by a force equal to its static thrust. Are the two speeds really the same? If not, why not?

n. Then there are the purely practical problems, such as what weights are needed? How is the towing line attached? How can you empty the guttering? (Do not try to lift one end.)

This list of problems that might be tackled is by no means exhaustive. They are, with the exception of *n*, arranged in order of difficulty.

---

*This is far more difficult than it sounds as the force is small, and if pulleys are used there is friction trouble.

2.3 Wakes and waves

Any object passing through a fluid causes a disturbance. Sometimes the disturbance is smooth and predictable; on other occasions it is broken and not so predictable. (This is an over-simplification, because often streamlined flow can give rise to vortices as, for example, at the tips of aeroplane wings.) When a vessel moves on the surface of water, waves are set up. In a similar way, anything moving through the air sets up waves.

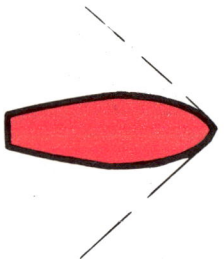

It would be interesting to examine the bow waves set up by boats moving through water. In general, these waves form a V if looked at from above. Is there a connection between the speed of the boat and the angle of the V? How can the waves be reduced? What

A model of a nuclear submarine undergoing tests in an 890 ft long tank at the Admiralty Experimental Works, Haslar, Gosport. Rough sea conditions and the effects of speeds of up to 30 knots are simulated to determine the best designs for hull and propellers

shapes produce fewer or smaller waves? How can the waves be recorded? Could a camera be mounted vertically above the gutter? Could an electronic flash unit be used to freeze the motion of the boat and waves? Are waves reflected from the sides of the gutter? Does the angle of reflection equal the angle of incidence?

To show surface movements try: *a.* sawdust; *b.* aluminium powder; *c.* drops of ink.

If an 8 mm cine camera is available, try to make a film record of the work.

Make hulls of different shapes from balsa wood and expanded polystyrene. The following shapes of hulls could be tested:

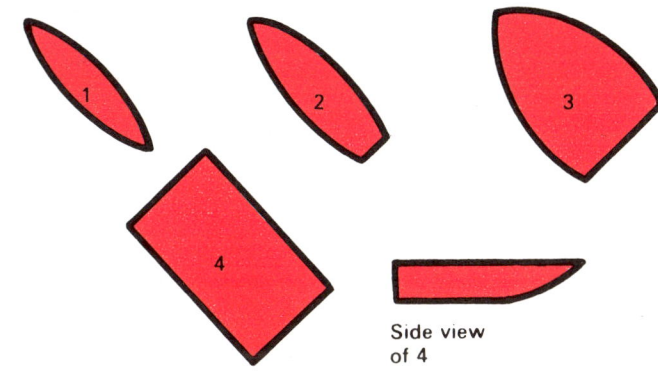

2.4 Testing a streamlined hull

Make a series of shapes from $2 \times \frac{1}{2}$ in [51 × 13 mm] wood.

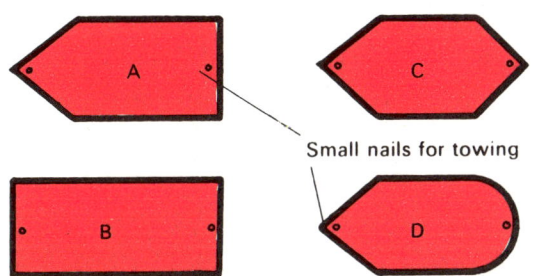

Make them so that they all have the same over-all weight.

Tow them using different towing forces and record their times over a set distance. Plot the times against force on the same graph paper. Are there any surprises? Do any of the curves cross one another? What does this mean?

Besides the times, record anything you notice about the behaviour of the boats. Sometimes the results are so surprising that children could be asked to arrange shapes *A, B, C, D* in order of speed before they try them; this could take place during a discussion on streamlining.

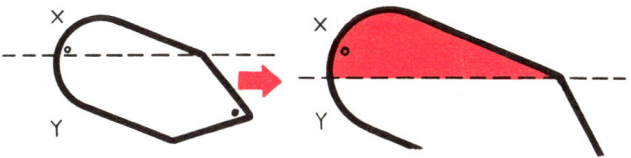

Shape *D* will inevitably snake as it is towed along unless it is fitted with a rudder. The reason for this is that when the boat yaws slightly the portion of the stern marked *X* acts as an 'airfoil' section to a greater effect than that marked *Y*, with the result that the yaw is increased until a stall is produced, and the yaw-producing force suddenly diminishes. The stern swings back, overshoots and a yaw-producing force is established in the opposite direction. Of the shapes shown, it is most likely that *A* will be the steadiest and fastest. A cut-off stern like this is called a trawler stern and is often used on short dumpy boats as it has a number of useful properties.

Does a long thin boat with a rounded stern snake as badly as one which has the same beam but is shorter?

Construct different-shaped hulls from expanded polystyrene; as far as possible make them all the same

The action of an 'airfoil' section.

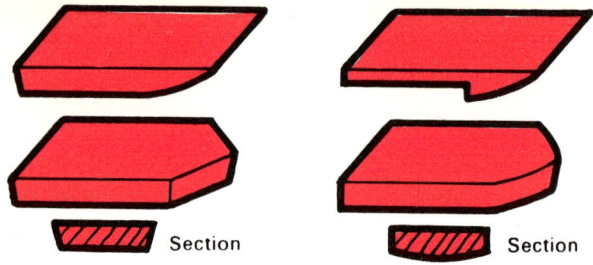

Examples of shapes to try

maximum width and length. Is there any difference in their performance? Try using larger towing forces.

A useful tool for cutting polystyrene is a hot-wire tile cutter obtainable from a decorator's shop. The cutter is intended to be run from a 4·5 V battery, but the current consumption soon runs the battery flat, so use either a low-voltage power pack or battery charger. If a charger is used, make a ballast resistance (about 3 Ω) out of resistance wire (26 swg Constantan is quite suitable, other gauges and types of wire will do provided the wire does not get too hot). The cutting wire is easily broken but can be readily replaced by 36 swg iron wire (1 oz reels from British Drug Houses) or 34 swg Constantan.

2.5 Follow-up

This work on boats can lead quite naturally to the movement in water of animals, to shape and size, and to fluid flow.

Nuffield Combined Sciences *Teacher Guide II* has a subsection developing these ideas (pages 27–53), and the work on boats could lead into more formal work quite easily. Of particular interest is the section 'Looking at shape and movement through water' using the Fluid Flow Model (Nuffield item no. 332 available from A. M. Lock Ltd, 79 Union Street, Oldham, Lancs.). This is a small metal tank with a glass bottom. A flow of water is generated by rotating paddles, and if the model is placed on an overhead projector and light shone through it on to a screen, the water flow around various shapes can be studied.

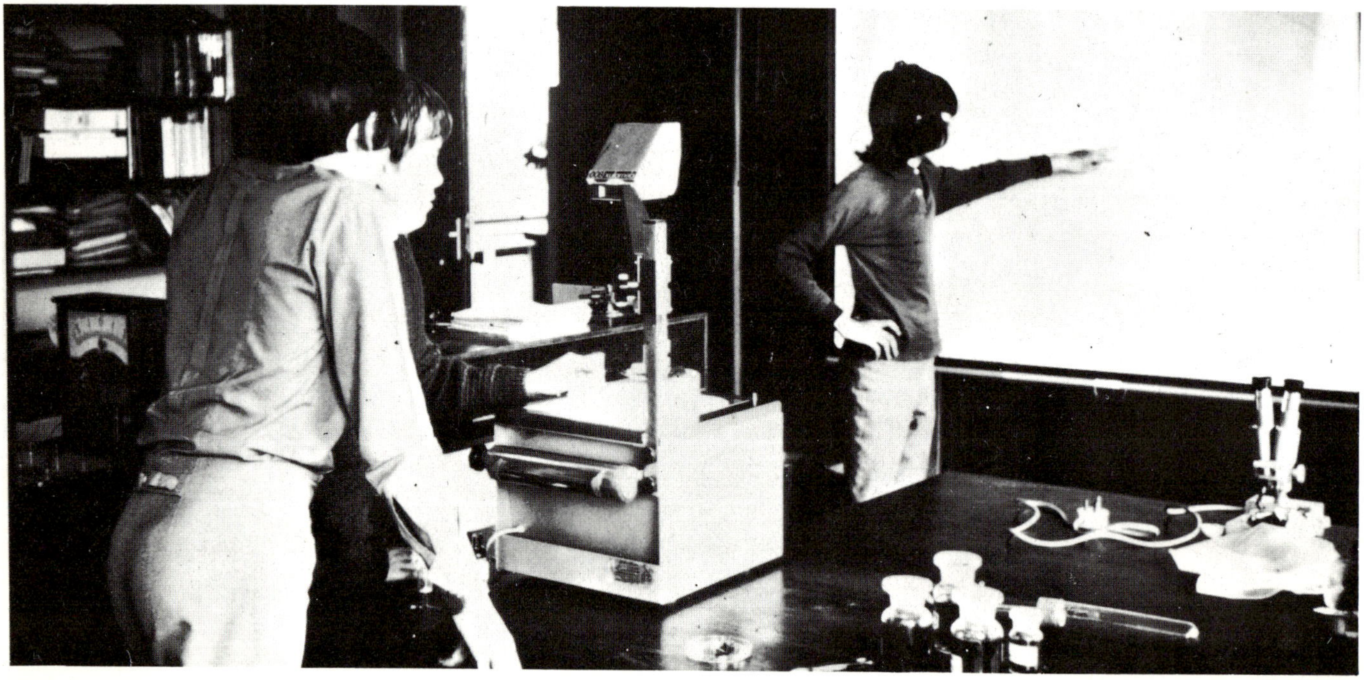

2.6 Motors

Type	Use
Elastic motors	Simple, easily home-made, see *Science from toys Stages 1 and 2*.
Electric motors	Very common shop toys.
Diesel or glow-plug engines	Home-made boats.
Steam engines	An engine suitable for driving a boat will now have to be made. This is not so difficult and most juniors could make one in the school metal workshop (see section 2.11).
Clockwork motors	Although the motors are not available it is sometimes possible to buy a clockwork boat.

What work can develop from motors?

2.7 Elastic motors

Investigations are of two kinds: *a.* those which involve the performance of the whole motor; *b.* those which are concerned with the elastic itself.

2.7.1 Investigations with the motor
How long does the motor run? How can you make the motor run longer? Does doubling the length of elastic double the duration of run?

Start using two strands.

Now double the length, still two strands.

Double the length, but make four strands.

Note how the elastic is doubled.

Would gears help? After all, a number of toys contain gears.

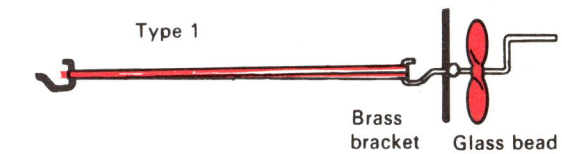

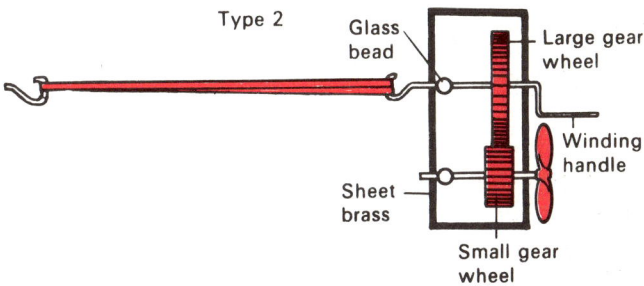

Which runs the longer, type 1 or type 2? Does each arrangement give the same amount of push to the boat?

This would involve making two identical hulls, fitting one with type 1 and the other with type 2. Then either measure the speed of each boat or measure their static thrusts (see page 13).

Does the static thrust remain constant as the motor runs down?

Try different thicknesses/widths of strip elastic, starting with the thinnest available ($\frac{1}{8}$ in [3 mm] square or thinner).

Devise and construct a gearing system to drive twin propellers.

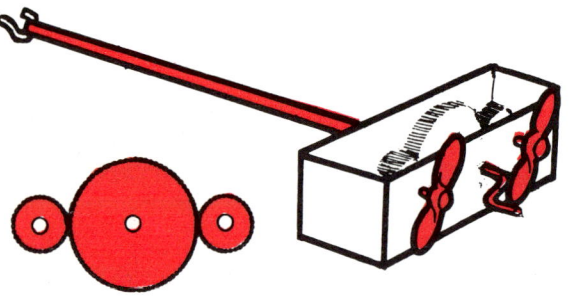

Try different sizes and pitch (twist) of propellers. What effects do they have on speed and duration of run? What is the effect of torque on the model?* What model shape is least affected by torque?

Energy is required to cause movement. Where does the energy come from to drive an elastic-powered boat? How is it stored?

The *Solarbo Book of Balsa Models* gives details of simple boats which can be powered by elastic motors.

2.7.2 Investigations into the properties of rubber

The main property we are interested in is the elasticity of rubber—its ability to be deformed and then to resume its original shape when the deforming force is removed. By how much can you stretch a thin elastic band before it breaks? Try bands which seem to be made of different types of rubber. To avoid introducing more than one variable at a time, make sure that the bands

---

*Some children found that they had to add outriggers to their boats to prevent them from turning over.

are the same size. Try different-sized bands of the same material. Are green bands as strong as red bands?

By how much do bands stretch? How do we measure stretch? Should it be a length or a percentage increase? Is there any connection between the cross-sectional area of an elastic band and the fractional or percentage increase in its length under a given load? Try bands of the same length but different thickness/width.

In these investigations it would be unwise to rely upon the results from one elastic band. In what way does chance affect our investigations?

Take one elastic band, load it and measure its extension using different loads until the band breaks. Plot your results on a graph. Is a part of your graph a straight line? Can you draw any conclusions?

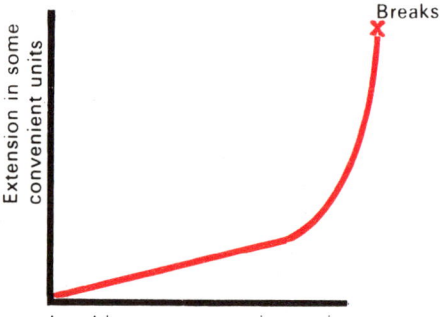

The extension could be measured directly in mm or cm or perhaps more conveniently, when dealing with bands of different length, as a percentage of the original length.

Take a long thin elastic band and keep loading it until it is loaded to about half its breaking point. Measure its extension. Now put the whole apparatus into a warm place, eg an electric oven at 50°C. Leave it for a while and then examine the extension. Has it altered? What would be the effect of putting the apparatus in a refrigerator? Try it.

Take a long thin elastic band and load it until it is extended to about eighty percent of the way to its breaking point. Measure the extension. Now leave the apparatus set and undisturbed for several days. Re-examine the extension. Has it increased? If the band has broken, repeat using a lighter load. Remove the load and compare the length of the band with its original length. The change is known as creep.

2.8 Electric motors

Cheap, low-voltage electric motors are available from model shops. Many mechanical toys are powered by them. A study of simple electricity and magnetism could be initiated by considering such a motor (see *Change Stage 3*, section 3.2.1). The storage and generation of electrical energy could also be investigated and studied (see *Change Stage 3*, sections 8.3.1 and 8.3.2).

2.9 Diesel or glowplug engines

These are small internal combustion engines, generally of between $\frac{1}{2}$ and 10 cc capacity, which produce anything up to $1\frac{1}{4}$ hp (a sewing machine motor is usually $\frac{1}{40}$ hp). A family car engine is 'revving' well if it does 5000 rev/min. Some of these little motors go up to 25 000 rev/min.

An enthusiast will be able to find a lot of science in these engines—the tyro is most likely to be put off. However, if there are any enthusiasts around, it would be worth getting them to explain to the rest of the class how the engines work.

The *Keil Kraft Handbook* (published annually) usually has a section on diesel or glowplug engines, explaining how they work and giving hints on starting and maintenance (see page 20).

The 'revs' of these engines can be measured in various ways. The simplest method is to use a resonance rev-counter which works on the principle that a length of wire or spring will oscillate at a fixed frequency dependent on the length, and the motor will oscillate at a certain frequency dependent on its speed. The counter holder is held in contact with the motor, and the length of wire is altered until the wire reaches its maximum oscillation. Comparatively inexpensive.

A more complicated method is to shine a light at the propellor and measure the frequency of the pulses of reflected light by a photo-transistor. The electronic circuit is similar to that used in the rev-counters in many GT motor cars.

Another method is to use an adjustable stroboscope, but it is easy to get harmonics (ie multiples) of the true figure particularly if the instrument does not cover the speed range of the motor.*

2.10 Steam engines

About the only time a steam engine is likely to be seen in a model boat is if the engine and the boat are home-made. It is not difficult to make an oscillating cylinder steam engine, particularly if the help of the metalwork department can be enlisted. Complete details of how to make a simple engine are given in *Model Engineering for Schools Book 1: Steam Engine and Boiler,* by T. E. Haynes (John Murray). The author says that it is well within the capability of a pupil in the junior forms of a secondary school. Certainly a steam engine could

---

A two-bladed propeller gives a figure of twice the true revs, unless one blade is painted white and the other black.

KNOW YOUR ENGINE!

What's that thingummyjig on the front of my engine? The truth of the matter is that although in most cases they agree, manufacturers often give different names to engine parts. So your thingummyjig may be a Spraybar or it may be a Jet Tube. We have prepared the following diagram to show the parts of a typical diesel or glowmotor and have used names and alternative names that are in general use today. If you do not have an illustrated parts list with your engine you will find the drawing useful, particularly when obtaining spares.

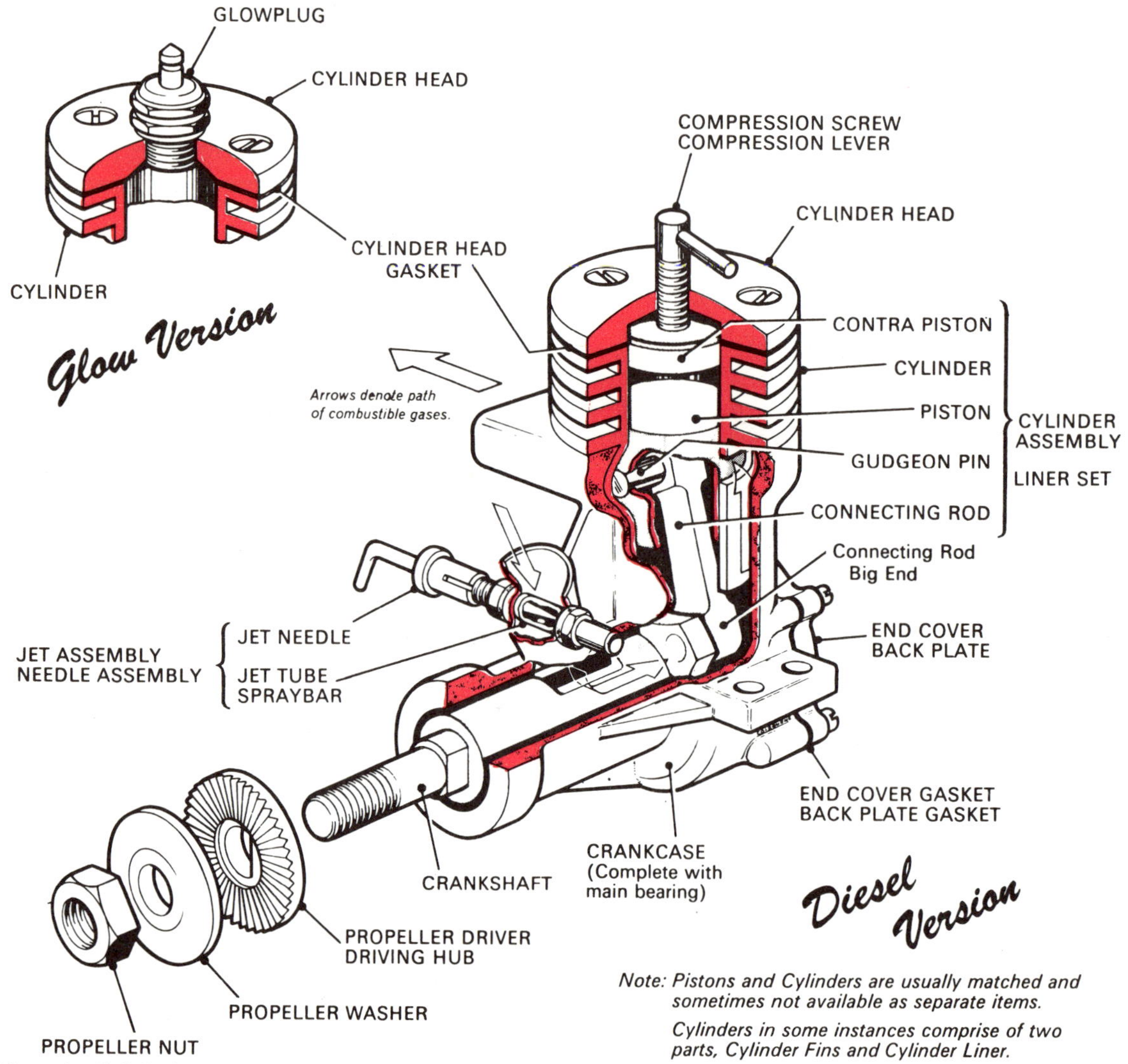

Reproduced from the *Keil Kraft Handbook*, 1970, by kind permission of E. Keil & Co Ltd, Wickford, Essex

be used as a start for the study of fuels, friction, energy, work and horse-power, besides being an opportunity for blending science and craftwork. The historical side of steam-driven boats could be studied—see *Change Stage 3*, section 3.2.2.

2.11 Clockwork motors

Like steam engines, these seem to be a thing of the past. Indeed, clockwork toys are becoming scarce, which is a great pity for they can be used for such topics as storing energy, mechanical systems and gearings, speed regulators.

2.12 Flotation

Sometime during a science course Archimedes' principle is bound to turn up. The understanding of this principle requires the prior development of the concept of volume conservation, and unless this is done then the principle cannot be properly understood.

Often this is covered up by a pupil learning parrot fashion. He can recite the words of the principle; he can work out problems by following a set procedure; but he does not understand what he is doing.

Perhaps some form of diagnosis should be made to find out whether a pupil accepts the concept of volume conservation before dealing with Archimedes' principle. It seems that a possible hierarchy of development might be the acceptance by a pupil:

a. That the volume of a given amount of water does not alter if it is poured into vessels of different shapes, or even if it is soaked up by blotting paper, or rags, or sand. (Temperature constant, of course.)

b. That the total volume is not altered no matter into how many different portions the volume is divided.

c. That if an object is completely immersed in a liquid, the volume of the liquid displaced is equal to the volume of the object.

d. That if an object is only partly immersed in a liquid, the volume of liquid displaced is only equal to the volume of the object which lies below the surface of the liquid.

e. That when an object of weight *Xg* is at rest on something then that something 'pushes back' with a force equal to *Xg*. (This implies a previous acceptance that a body of weight *Xg* has a downward force acting on it of *Xg*.)

f. Later, it might be well to consider how the supporting force acts on the surface of a body. Is there a supporting force from the water acting on an oil tanker firmly aground on a sandbank, even if the tide rises? Is there a supporting force from the water acting on a wood pile driven into the sea bottom?

g. That the supporting force of the liquid is equal to the weight of liquid displaced.

h. That when an object is completely immersed there is still some form of supporting force.

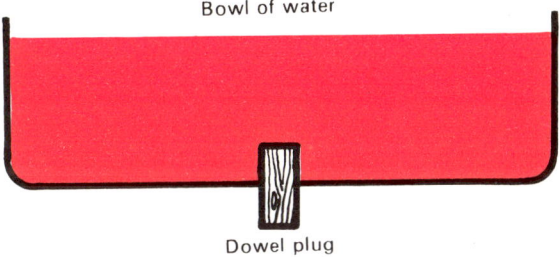

Is there an upthrust on the dowel plug?

i. That a body 'loses' weight when immersed in a liquid. (Does it lose mass?)

j. That the 'loss' in weight is equal to the weight of the liquid displaced.

All these form a nice set of logical deductions, easy enough if you are trained in science but, quite frankly, beyond most children at the age of eleven or twelve years. The result is that they learn how to present an answer which is acceptable rather than one based on understanding.

Can we use boats (and balls, which on the beach inevitably seem to end up in the sea) to provide experiences of flotation? Can we start with model boat displacements? Can we measure the volume of displaced water?

Suppose Plasticine cubes were made, their volumes calculated and the cubes dropped one by one into a measuring cylinder containing water. The displaced volumes could be read off directly. How accurately could the work be carried out? For pupils who know, or think they know, what the answer is, the errors involved can be studied. How accurately can the solids be made? How accurately can the volume of water be measured?

What displaced volume would be expected in the previous experiment if all the Plasticine cubes were

a. Compressed into one cube?

b. Compressed into one sphere?

c. Compressed into one irregular shape?

The difference between floating boats in sea water rather than river water could be investigated in the classroom and outside (swimming and Plimsoll lines). This could lead to making a drinking straw hydrometer (see *Change Stages 1 and 2*) and using it to measure not density but the concentration of a salt solution.

A model submarine submerges not because it weighs more than the water it displaces but because it relies on hydroplanes (H) to control its floating and submerging. These work in a similar way to the ailerons (A) and elevators (E) of an aircraft. It is worth noting that the hydroplanes of a submarine and the elevators and ailerons of an aircraft act on a fluid, and that sometimes water and air behave in a similar manner. Hydrodynamics and aerodynamics are similar sciences; the main difference between them is that water is virtually incompressible, whereas with air we have to make allowances for its compressibility.

2.13 Sources of materials

a. Six-inch [152 mm] plastics guttering—builders' merchants.

b. Washers—Meccano.

c. Plastics pulleys—model shops.

d. Hot-wire polystyrene cutter—decorators' shop.

e. 36 swg iron wire—British Drug Houses. Constantan wire—laboratory suppliers.

f. Elastic for motors, sold in different widths: $\frac{1}{8}$ in, $\frac{3}{16}$ in, $\frac{1}{4}$ in—model shops (supplies of metric equivalents may be difficult to obtain).

g. Electric motors—suitable motors are made by Orbit and distributed by Ripmax.

They, or motors similar to them, can be obtained from model shops. A cheap source of electric motors is the Modellers' Den, 2 Lower Boro' Walls, Bath BA1 1QR.

h. Gear wheels, piano wire, propellers, balsa wood, diesel

Orbit electric motor data

	Orbit 305	Orbit 405	Orbit 505
Normal voltage	1·5 V	3 V	3 V
Voltage range	1·5–3 V	1·5–6 V	1·5–6 V
Torque at normal voltage	15–30 g cm*	55–75 g cm*	70–85 g cm*
Rev/min at normal voltage	5500–6500	8500–10 500	7000–9000
Current consumption at normal voltage	200–300 mA	200–300 mA	200–300 mA
Weight	39 g	53 g	68 g
Shaft diameter	2·3 mm	2·3 mm	2·3 mm

and glowplug-motors and fuel—all from model shops.

i. A very useful book containing know-how on modelling is the *Keil Kraft Handbook,* which is published annually. It also has a catalogue section.

j. Adhesives. There are so many 'glues' available to modellers that a choice may seem to be a matter of hit and miss. However, a knowledge of their properties is needed to make sure that a suitable choice is made:

*What are the SI Units for torque?

Balsa cement
Usually a cellulose derivative dissolved in suitable solvents (acetone, MEK, esters). It is quick-drying, and useful for glueing paper, card and balsa wood. The slower-drying varieties will glue hardwoods. None of these is suitable for boats unless waterproofed with varnish.

Casein glues
Bought in powder form. When mixed with cold water it gives a glue which forms strong joints in woodwork if the wood is held together under pressure. Joints are moisture resistant but not waterproof.

Cascamite
Sold as a powder. It is prepared by mixing with water. It does not set by evaporation but by a chemical reaction. Once set, the glue is waterproof.

PVA (polyvinyl-acetate)
This is a white emulsion without the usual tackiness of glue. A very suitable glue for *all* woods, paper and card, but not suitable for boats or where the finished product is subjected to damp conditions. It is useful when a longer working time is needed to enable parts to be moved. It dries out almost transparent.

Evo-stik woodworking adhesive
Another 'white' glue.

Epoxy resin
For example, Araldite, Devcon, Britfix 88. More expensive than other glues but will join almost anything to anything provided the surfaces are dry and not greasy. When set the glue is insoluble in solvents. Setting and curing times vary considerably from five minutes to a week—much depends on the temperature and the make of the adhesive. Devcon is the fastest of the commonly available brands. It is obtainable through model shops.

Polystyrene cement
Only suitable for polystyrene sheet *not* expanded polystyrene, eg ceiling tiles.

3 Balls

3.1 Stage 1, 2 and 3 work

In *Science from toys,* the variables (factors) influencing the bouncing of balls are discussed and likely investigations proposed. The investigations are mainly confined to Stages 1 and 2, although some Stage 3 work is indicated. *Before Stage 3 work is started, children should have the opportunity to try the earlier Stages, particularly if the work is new to them.* Simple investigations could include:

1. Making a collection of balls of different sizes, weights and materials. Use such a collection for simple measurements. Is the biggest ball the heaviest? How can you measure the diameter of a ball?

2. How high does a ball bounce? How can you measure it? If you compare the bounce of one ball with another, how can you make sure that your comparison is fair?

3. Does the surface on which you bounce the ball have any effect on the height of bounce? Try different surfaces. How can the results be recorded and displayed?

Stage 3 work is mainly directed towards:

a. Energy—or, more simply, the 'go' of things.

b. The mathematical connection between the height of drop and the height of bounce.

c. The mechanism of bouncing.

Throughout the investigations, the theme of variables constantly arises, and these can be examined (see Objectives 1.42, 1.44, 2.42, 2.43, 3.32 on page 94) to an ever-increasing degree of sophistication.

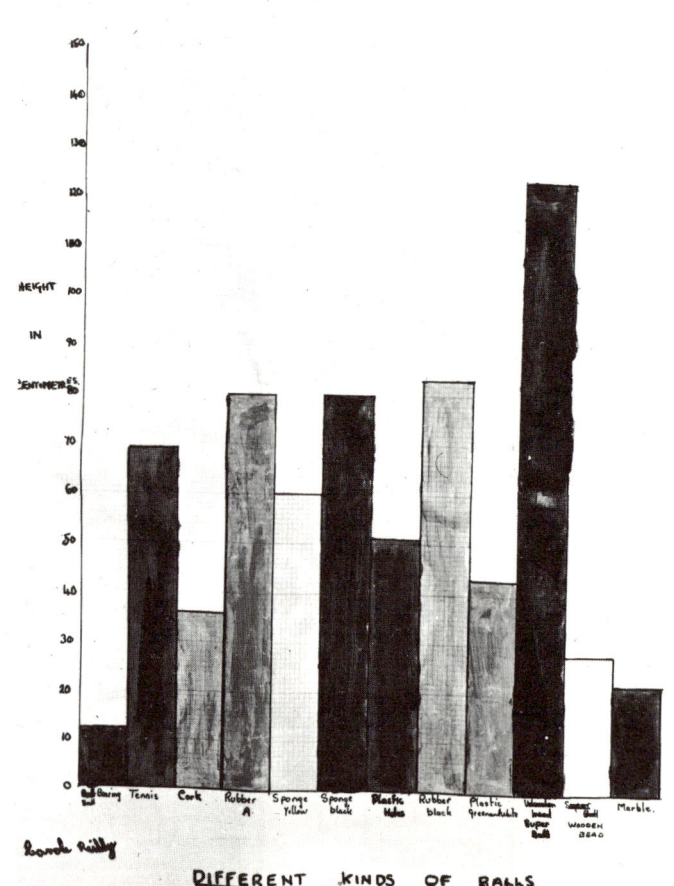

3.2 Energy and the mechanics of bouncing

Energy was defined by Clerk Maxwell as being the 'go' of things. Now this 'go' has many forms, and discussions with children have shown that they primarily associate it with a breakfast food! 'Something gives you energy', 'So and so is energetic', 'I haven't got the energy to . . .'. Energy is a common word which has a wide range of meanings, and it is its common usage with which pupils will be familiar. We need constantly to ask, 'What is it which makes it go?' If we hold a ball and then let go, what makes the ball go?

At Stages 1 and 2 children equate the properties of a substance with the substance: they are unable to divorce properties (abstract) from substance (concrete).

This makes it impossible to talk about 'energy', on its own, because 'energy' is an abstract concept and is meaningless to Stage 1 or 2 children unless it is paired with something concrete. In this case, energy and ball are paired so discussion can be started at an earlier stage and the level raised until for Stage 3 children 'energy' becomes an abstraction.

We need to distinguish between potential energy, or energy of position, and kinetic energy, ie between energy which is available but not doing anything, and the energy of actually going from one place to another, the energy of movement. If we can establish during discussions that energy can bring about changes and that change takes place as a result of the interaction of energy with something else, then perhaps children who have reached Stage 3 could complete a work card or sheet something like the following.

3.2.1 Sample work-sheet: energy and bouncing balls

Note. This sheet is intended for children who have reached Stage 3, not for those who are still in Stages 1 or 2. This is only a suggested work-sheet: it may not suit your class or your ideas.

Work Sheet: ENERGY AND BOUNCING BALLS

1   What kind of energy does a ball have if it is held at A? . . . .

2   The ball is dropped and is just about to touch the floor at B; what kind of energy does it most have now? . . . .

3   The ball has been dropped and has reached C; what kinds of energy does it have now? . . . .

4   If a ball is dropped onto a hard surface does the shape of the ball change? . . . .

If it does change, is it a permanent or a temporary change? . . . .

Try dropping a rubber ball and a ball of Plasticine.

Draw the final shape of a lump of Plasticine which has been dropped onto a hard floor -

Does Plasticine bounce? . . . .

Now try dropping it on an expanded polystyrene tile, does it bounce? . . . .

To explain why, we need to carry out an investigation into 'Bouncing'

5 Using the same ball and the same surface on which to drop it find out how the height of bounce varies with the height of dropping.

Plot your results on the graph.

6 Using the small ball and the same height of dropping but different surfaces on which to drop it, find out how the height of bounce varies.

Try a wooden floor, concrete floor, expanded polystyrene tile, tray of sand.

Are there any changes in the surfaces on which you drop the ball?

....

....

How is the energy involved in the changes?

....

....

Where does this energy come from?

....

....

7 If a rubber ball is dropped onto a hard surface, the shape is temporarily flattened: a change has taken place.

Where has the energy come from?

....

For a brief instant of time the ball is at rest, has it any energy of movement? ....

Where has this energy gone? ....

Why does the ball bounce? ....

8 A ball at rest at A is dropped and by the time it reaches B has gained 10 units of energy of movement. Suppose you wanted to throw this ball from B to A, how many units of energy of movement would you have to give it?

....

If you provided only 8 units of energy of movement what effect would this have?

....

....

9 If the ball is dropped from A and bounces to C, what can you say about the energies of movement, just BEFORE it touches B; just AFTER it bounces off B?

....

10 Fill in the following summary:

A ball held at A has energy of........................; *as the ball falls this energy is changed into*..........
.... *Upon hitting the floor the energy of*........................ *may be used to*
.... *the ball, make a*........................ *in the floor, make a*........................
which you can hear. If the energy which has been used to........................ *the ball or*............
.... *the floor is given back quickly enough the ball will bounce and the height to which it bounces*
will depend on the amount of energy which is returned.

11 Obtain a 'medium' or 'slow' squash ball; drop it from 2m and record the height to which it bounces. Do this several dozen times. Are all the heights the same or is there some progression in results?

Warm the ball by putting it on the radiator for some time, then carry out the bouncing test. Is the bounce height the same as it was when the ball was cold?

Explain: (a)   your results

(b)   why it is necessary to 'knock up' before starting a squash game.

12 What variables are concerned with the bouncing of a ball?

Comment on each of the following:

THE BALL

Size: ....

Shape: ....

Weight: ....

Material of which it is made: ....

Colour: ....

Height from which it is dropped: ....

Any others? ....

THE SURFACE ON WHICH IT IS DROPPED

Material of which it is made: ....

Roughness/Smoothness: ....

Rigidity of the surface: ....

13 Complete the following:

When a lump of Plasticine is dropped onto a hard surface the energy of movement is used up in changing..........
.... *When the Plasticine is dropped onto an elastic surface some of the energy of movement is*
used up in........................ *this energy is given back to the Plasticine and caused it to*......
....

27

3.2.2 Summary

There is considerable confusion over elasticity and bouncing, particularly if the bouncing of a rubber ball on a large smooth lump of steel is compared with the bouncing of a steel ball-bearing on the same surface. The explanation of such similarity is best left until pupils have some knowledge of the particulate nature of matter and are able to divorce a property from the substance having that property. However, in general, bouncing can be explained using simple energy ideas, eg, when a ball hits a surface, some of the energy of movement deforms the surface, the ball, or both. If the energy is given back quickly enough then the ball bounces. Some rubber balls bounce better than others—why? This depends on two factors:

a. The speed with which the energy is handed back.

b. Whether all the energy is returned or some is lost, eg, in making a noise or warming the ball.

These ideas can be easily followed by a child who is ready for them but unless he is ready they would only be learnt, not understood.

3.3 The connection between the height of drop and the height of bounce

If we drop a ball 2 m and it bounces 1·5 m, how high will it bounce if it is dropped 3 m?

Already children are used to carrying out investigations and graphing the results, so if the question is posed during a group discussion they will most likely give a method for finding out even if they cannot actually drop the ball 3 m. Change the question slightly: is there any connection between the height of bounce and the height of drop? This is a tough question for all but the very able; some children may be able to see simple relationships, for example:

Dropped from 1·60 m, bounces 1·20 m

Dropped from 0·16 m, bounces 0·12 m

But the relationship

Height of bounce = height of drop × $\frac{3}{4}$

is most likely to be beyond many children. If it is, it should not be pressed but can be taken up later.

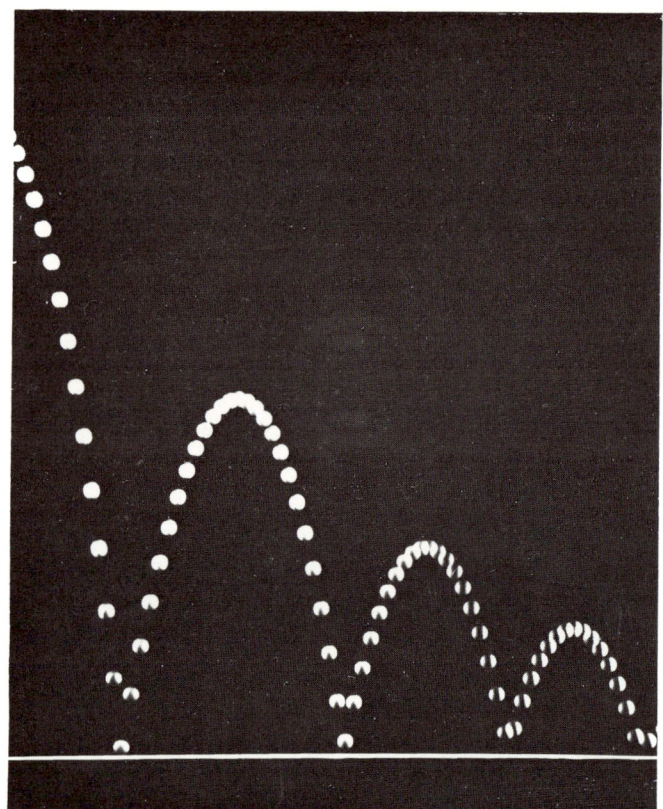

3.4 Rolling balls down slopes

Children are fond of running toy cars and trucks down slopes, racing one against another.* Instead of using toy cars, suppose balls are tried. Will big balls run down slopes as fast as, or faster than, small ones? There are many practical problems, for example:

*How many boys play this in their first two years at secondary school? What do your children play with? Can you make use of their interest?

a. How can we make sure that each ball travels the same distance?

b. How can we time each ball?

c. Does the weight of the ball influence the speed?

Work on these lines could be carried out in the classroom using a plank of wood and balls of various kinds. There are some factors which children at this stage cannot investigate but which teachers need to consider:

a. A solid ball has a different moment of inertia from a hollow ball. Will this influence the time taken for the balls to roll down the slope? (Assume both balls have the same weight.)

b. What effect has friction on the rolling?

c. What effect does the softness of the ball have on its speed?

Ball-bearings of different sizes can be rolled down a slope made from the H-channelling that is used as a curtain rail. This needs to be kept immaculately clean because specks of dust act as boulders to small ball-bearings.

Make a toy in which ball-bearings are rolled down a curtain rail, shot into the air to land in a tin. Ask children to get the ball-bearings in the tin. What variables can they alter to vary either the trajectory or range of the ball-bearings?

4 Ballista—mangonel*

A model of a medieval mangonel made from firewood by a boy of ten. As far as possible, this is an accurate reconstruction of a full-size engine.

A model made from easily obtainable materials. This model can be used for the investigations outlined in section 4.2.

The ballista and the mangonel were ancient siege weapons used to throw stones and shoot arrows. The propulsive force was derived from the untwisting of ropes of hair. Do you remember the story of the siege of Syracuse, Archimedes, and women giving their hair to make ropes for the siege engines?

Syracuse, sea port and city of Sicily, was inhabited by Greek colonists before it was taken by the Romans. It had been successfully held against the Athenians in 414 BC, but just two hundred years later in the Second Punic War (the war in which Hannibal crossed the Alps) Syracuse was again besieged, this time by a Roman army under Marcellus.

*See II Chronicles, xxvi, 15.
A summary of the history, construction and effects in warfare of the projectile throwing engines of the ancients, *by Sir Ralph W. F. Payne-Gallwey, London, Longmans, 1907.*

It was during this siege that Archimedes designed various war machines, which considerably disorganised the Romans by their originality and unexpectedness. The ballista was used to provide a fixed line of fire so that if ships approached the city walls these engines were already sighted and could put down a curtain barrage. The ballista used the stored energy in ropes made of hair or gut, and it was for this purpose that the women of Syracuse gave their hair.

The city finally fell as the result of pestilence, famine and treachery. The popular account of its falling as the result of a surprise attack during a festival is not correct. It is true that such an attack was made, but it had only a very limited success confined to an outpost citadel. Archimedes was killed during the sack of the city by the Romans, supposedly because he refused to answer them when interrogated.

Until the early Middle Ages there were two ways of storing mechanical energy for use in weapons:

a. Bending flexible material—bows.

b. Twisting rope—ballista, mangonel, onager.

It was not until later that the falling of weights was used in a catapult (trebuchet).

In *Science from toys Stages 1 and 2*, some investigations are suggested for the mangonel. Some of them could be carried out with suitable refinements, and perhaps a larger-scale model could be made in the woodwork shop. Once again a chance for cooperation.

4.1 Measurements: length—accuracy/and approximation—an outline of a possible class discussion

To find the range of our mangonel, we need to measure the distance it throws something. That is, we have to measure lengths.

a. What do we use to measure length with?

b. What units can we use?

c. What is the value of each division on our measuring instrument?

d. What is the closest we can measure to?

e. If the 'distance mark' comes in between two calibration marks on our ruler, what can we do?

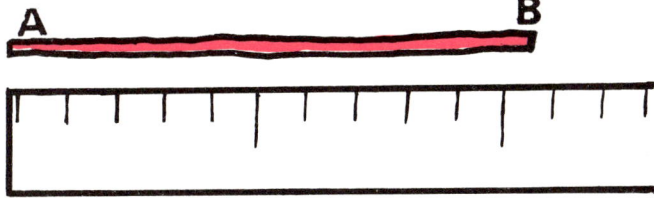

f. How wide is a sheet of writing paper? Is it an exact number of units on the ruler or is it between two calibration marks?

g. Suppose the length was 8·4 cm but we said that the length was 8 cm. By what amount have we under-measured the distance? What is the fraction by which we have under-measured it? If we said the measurement was 9 cm, by how much have we over-measured it?

h. How closely can you measure the width of a room?

i. How closely can you measure the range of our mangonel?

j. So far we have seen that measuring distances will depend on our *measuring instrument*.

k. Now suppose we ask thirty people to measure the same distance with the same instrument, will they all get the same figure? Try it. So the next factor we must take into consideration is *human error*. (When measuring we must avoid errors due to parallax as well as the misreading of numbers.)

4.2 The range of the mangonel

In *Science from toys, Stages 1 and 2** an investigation into the range of a mangonel is suggested and a pattern of hits illustrated. There is a scatter, not just one point on which all the shots would fall. This scatter appears to be random; there is not a constant error.

Before we go any further, we can say that the third factor in the measurement of range is *something to do with the apparatus which produces the effect we are trying to measure.*

What in the apparatus is likely to cause these variations?

One of the variables is likely to be variations in the weight of the cherry stones. How can cherry stones be

---

*Science from toys Stages 1 and 2 contains suggestions for Stage 1 and 2 work on this topic, and it is essential for pupils to start at Stage 1 before trying more sophisticated ideas.

weighed? Is it really necessary to find the weight of each stone?

A top-pan balance could be used to select pieces of ammunition having similar individual weights. Schools have used all sorts of ammunition: cherry stones, dried peas, dried beans of various sizes, Plasticine, and dried peas which have been soaked overnight in water. One school reported that the soaked peas were particularly successful because they left a mark when they landed on a sheet of white lining paper, so the hits were self-registering. A lot of work has been carried out on the recording of hits. Besides the self-registering method of soaked peas and white paper, cardboard boxes to catch the ammunition have been used. Trouble has been experienced because the ammunition tends to jump out of the boxes. This can be lessened by using a wad of cotton wool in each box.

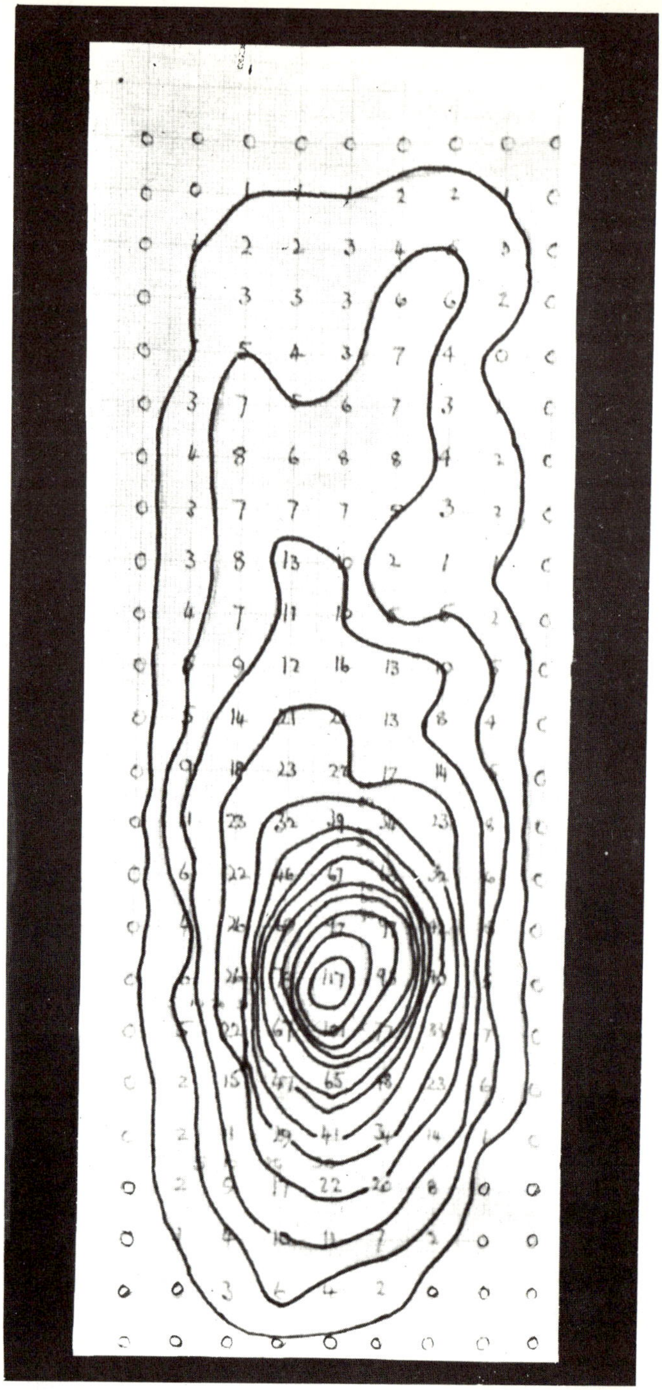

However the ammunition is selected, and by whatever method the hits are recorded, the pattern of shots from

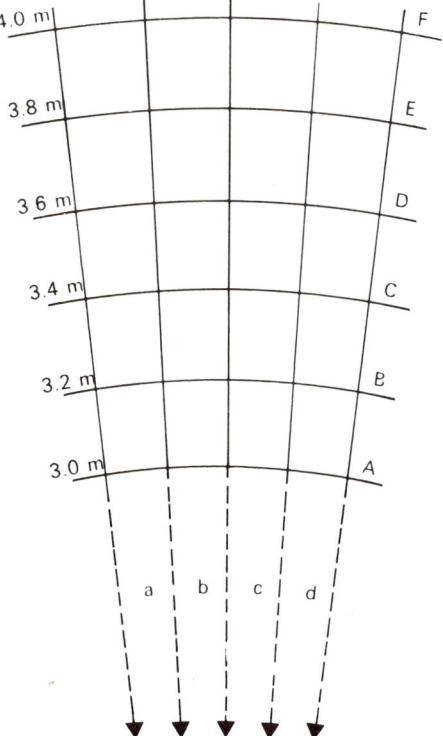

a matched group of pieces of ammunition could be compared with that from an unmatched group. Then, if there is a perceptible difference (for example, if the pattern is tighter and smaller) one effective variable has been recognised.

Can any other variables be recognised and investigated?

The measurement of range offers an opportunity for introducing some elementary statistics, eg introduction of the terms *mean, median, mode* and *frequency distribution*.

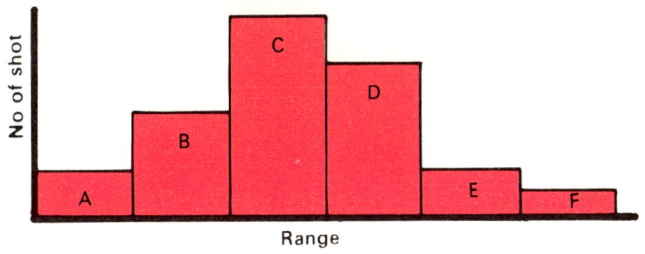

Histogram showing the frequency distribution of the shots

In the same way as the range can be investigated so can the angular dispersion be graphed.

There is no reason why a three-dimensional graph could not be constructed using drinking straws of different lengths to represent in the vertical plane the number of hits in each square. This is a practical application of some modern mathematics.

Another way of producing a three-dimensional graph is to record the hits in each square of 50 mm². Then draw a 'contour map' and use expanded polystyrene tiles to construct a solid graph.

4.3 Altering the range of the mangonel

What are the effective variables which are linked with the range? In other words, how can the range be altered? Things to try are:

a. Different weights of shot.

b. Different amounts of twist in the elastic bands.

c. The tilt of the mangonel.

d. The position of the two nails and band which stops the throwing arm.

e. The shape of the missile.

4.4. Energy

A stone flung by a mangonel has energy. From where does it get this energy? What happens to this energy? Can the energy which the stone has be given to something else? Is there any other way in which the energy could be 'lost'? If a lump of lead is hammered, the lead is flattened. What other effect is noticeable? (Children might have had the opportunity to try this for themselves.*) It is reasonable to suggest that when a stone is slowed down, some of its 'go' is 'lost' as heat. Suppose, instead of cherry stones, lead shot were used; and instead of one shot, lots were used; and instead of shooting them, they were allowed to fall, would they get hot?

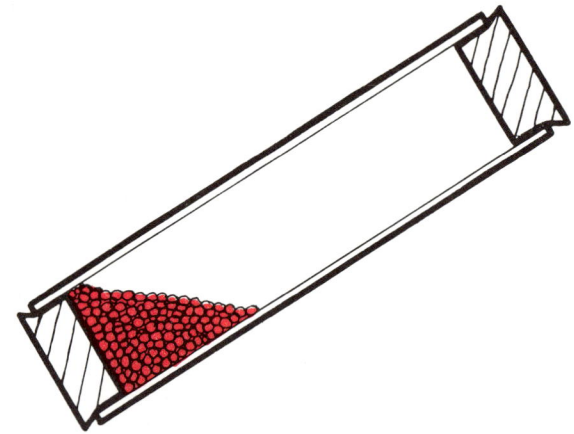

Take a long cardboard tube and fit a cork in one end. Immerse the bulb of a —5/+50° C 1/10° thermometer in lead shot contained in a 100 cm³ beaker. Leave the thermometer for several minutes and then read the temperature. Remove the thermometer and pour the lead shot into the tube. Cork the open end of the tube and invert the tube. Do this 100 times and then pour the shot back into the beaker and measure the temperature of the shot without delay.

In an investigation are we justified in performing an experiment once and taking only one set of results? Should we not carry out the determinations several times and take an average?

How much does the temperature rise? What would happen if twice the amount of shot were used? Try it and explain the results.✝

It is said that if a lead bullet with a velocity of 3·45 10⁴ cm/s is stopped and all its mechanical energy converted into heat, this heat will be enough to melt it (Edser, *Heat*, pages 286 and 474).

See Change Stage 3, section 3.3.1(*c*).
✝*Double the weight of the shot and the energy changes are doubled. But the double weight of material needs twice the amount of energy to raise it to the same temperature. Net result: the temperature rise is independent of the weight of shot.*

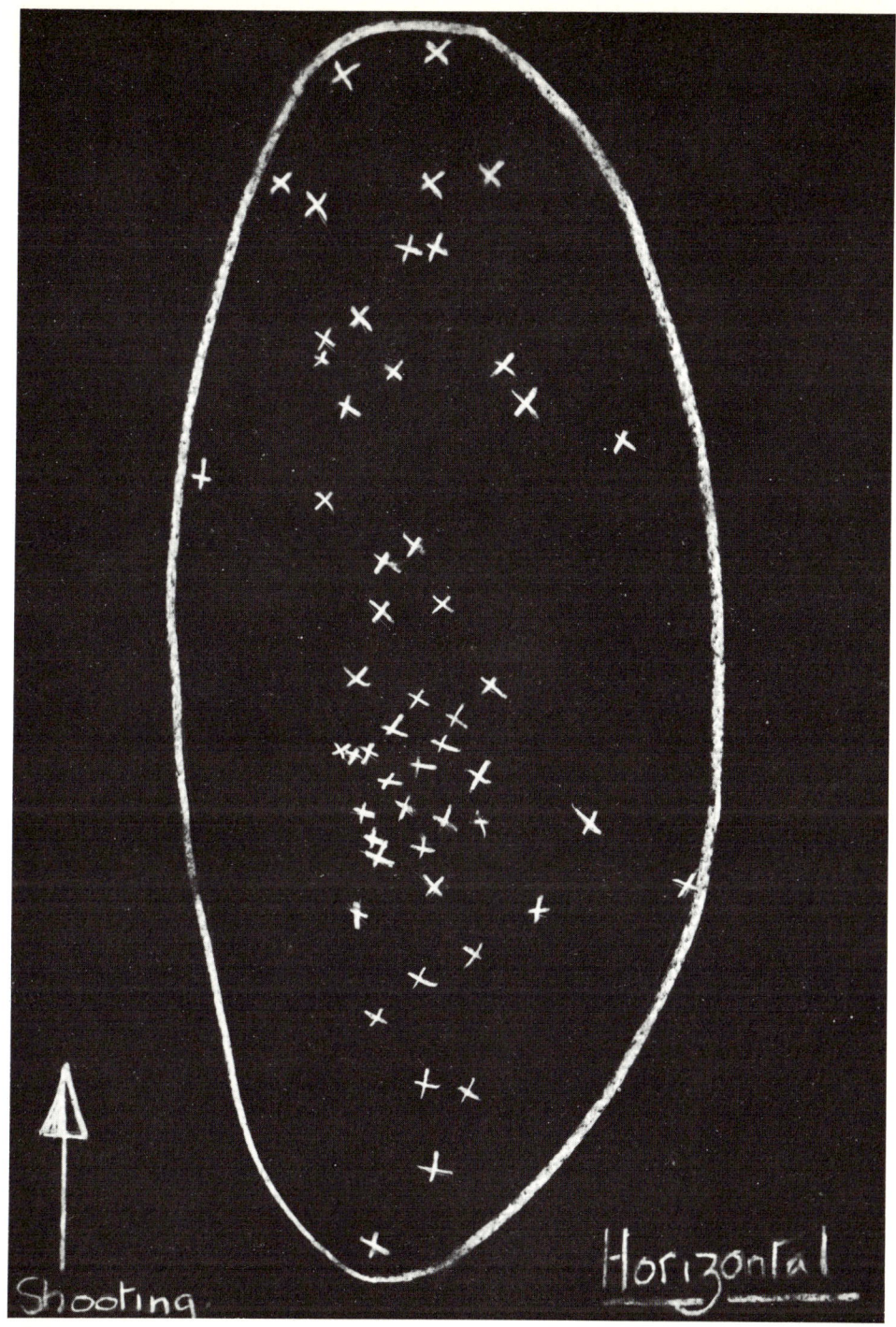

5 Cameras

5.1 What can we do using photographic materials?

The camera is a very popular 'toy' for pupils. It is so grown-up to own and use a camera that it is not regarded as a toy at all. Toy or not, it is a very useful tool in the hands of a teacher looking for a starting point, as the following flow chart shows.

5.1.1 Light-sensitive materials

Most pupils know that when a photograph is taken, something happens to the film. They accept it. It is a process, almost magic, which is far too 'complicated' for them to understand—or so they think. So it is relegated to the realms of those things which are accepted without question, like television and radio, nuclear power and penicillin. The camera becomes, in more senses than one, a black box. In work on photo-

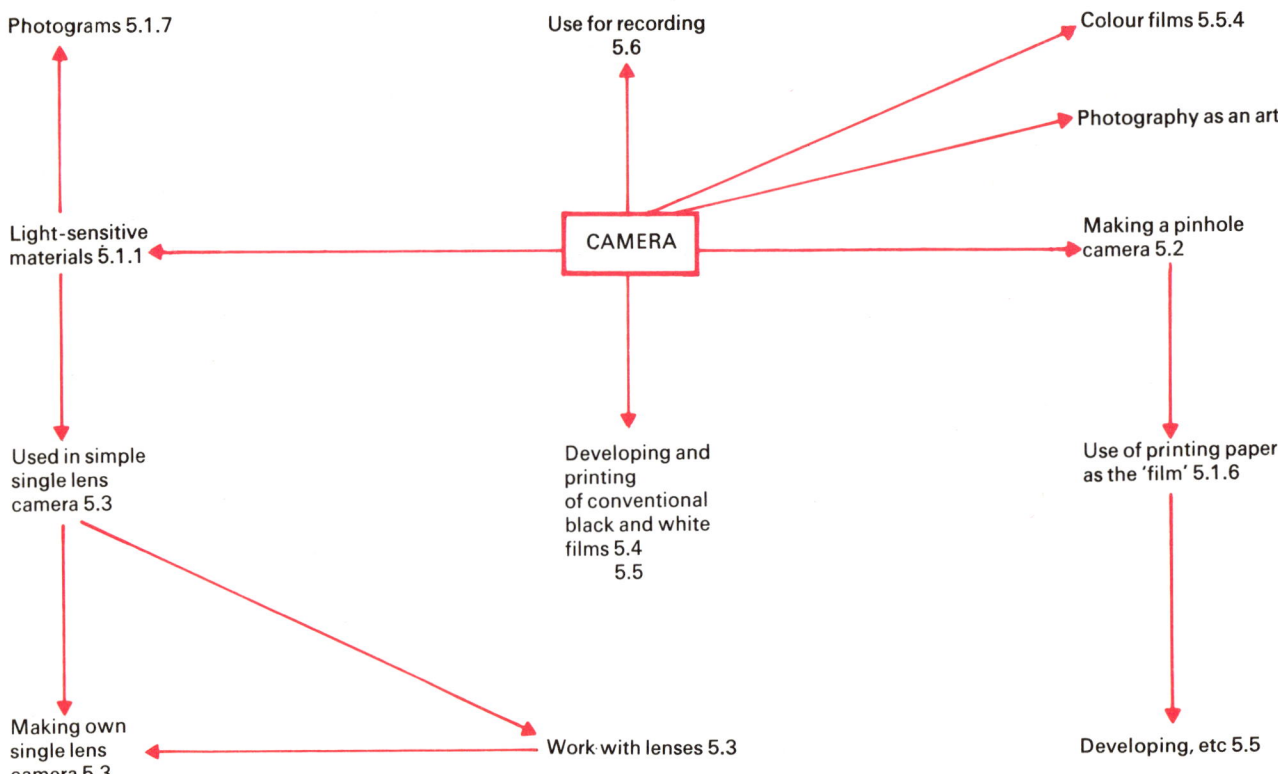

graphy, we aim to give pupils experiences that help them realise that light energy causes changes in a film.

Light-sensitive material	Change which takes place on exposure to light
Silver halides	a. Latent change not visible until the material is treated with chemicals (developers) which convert the changed material into silver. b. Visible changes, silver chloride changes from white to a grey-blue.
Blueprint material	Paper soaked in blueprint solution changes from a yellow-brown to blue, see section 5.1.3.
Gelatine and potassium dichromate	The gelatine becomes insoluble in water, see section 5.1.4.
Some dyes	They fade, eg, visual purple in the eye, colours of curtains.

The following article, by L. Gresswell (Havelock School, Grimsby), is reprinted by kind permission of Kodak Ltd, from *News for Education, Winter '70*.

5.1.2 Photo-silk-screen printing in a school

Photography is rapidly becoming established in the school curriculum as an art and craft in its own right. It can also form part of several allied processes that give scope for creative work. One such process is photo-silk-screen printing. This is a method by which a printed version of a photographic original can be applied to paper or other surfaces. The method outlined here can be employed in any school that is equipped for basic photography.

Stage 1. Preparation of the photographic image (In the darkroom)

First select the photograph that is to form the basis of the printed design. The negative chosen should have fairly high contrast. From this negative, make a contact print on 'Kodalith' Ortho Film, Type 3, (35 mm) to obtain a high-contrast positive. Make a second contact print from this positive, again using 'Kodalith' Ortho Film, to produce a high-contrast negative. Then use an enlarger to produce a positive image of the final size required, on a sheet of 'line' film (see note 1). The developer used in all these stages is a solution of 'Kodalith' Super Developer Powder, and the fixer is 'Kodafix' Solution. Use a 25 W safelamp fitted with a Kodak Safelight Filter No. 1A when handling 'Kodalith' Ortho Film.

Stage 2. Preparation of the sensitized silk screen

The screen is made by stretching nylon, terylene or silk over a rectangular wooden frame. To degrease the material, brush it with a 5% solution of caustic soda. When the screen has dried, in normal room lighting coat it on the inside with Seriset emulsion (see note 2). The emulsion is best applied with a piece of stiff card, using a scraping action to obtain a thin, even layer. Then leave the screen to dry *in the darkroom.*

Stage 3. Transferring the image to the screen

The screen is ready for exposure after two or three hours. Place the screen over a block of foam rubber, cut to fit just within the frame. Then take the sheet of 'line' film bearing the full-size positive image and place it with the emulsion side touching the outside of the screen. Hold it in contact with a sheet of clean glass. With the film and screen thus held in uniform contact, expose the screen to daylight through the film by placing it near a window for a period of 15 to 30 minutes, depending on the brightness of the day. After exposure, remove the glass and the film and immediately soak the screen in water. A negative image will soon become visible. Five minutes' soaking is sufficient for complete development. The process can be assisted by directing a jet of water at the screen. Allow the screen to dry overnight in a horizontal position.

Stage 4. The printing process

From this point, follow the normal silk-screen printing procedure: place the screen firmly in position over the surface to be printed, spread the screen ink as evenly as possible along one side of the screen, and use a rubber squeegee to sweep the ink across the screen with a firm smooth movement. A positive print is obtained.

There are several other ways of preparing the photographic image. For instance, instead of using cheap non-branded 'line' film, the full-size positive can be made in one step by enlarging from the original negative on to 'Kodalith' Ortho Film in sheet form. Alternatively, 'Kodalith' Translucent Paper, TP, can be used instead of the 'line' film. It is also possible to eliminate the negative stage by using an etch-bleach reversal process.

As a further variation a half-tone effect can be introduced using 'Kodalith' Autoscreen Ortho Film 2563 ('Estar' Base). Cut a piece of this film to the size of the chosen negative and make a half-tone positive by contact printing, then proceed in the manner described previously. The size of the dots, and hence the coarseness of the effect, will depend on the degree of enlargement involved in making the full-size positive. Interesting effects can be produced by using more than one colour; for example, out-of-register printing can produce a bas-relief or entirely abstract effect, depending on the degree of misregistration. At Havelock School we have also experimented with tone-separation by making high-contrast positives of different densities from the same original and using these to prepare screens for printing superimposed images in different colours. The photo-silk-screen process can be used for producing Christmas cards, tickets, posters, covers and illustrations for magazines, and other types of printed material. Children derive great enjoyment and satisfaction from the work, since they can produce results that have a 'professional' look while still retaining their personal stamp.

Materials needed
'Kodalith' Ortho Film 6556, Type 3
'Kodalith' Translucent Paper, TP, or 'line' film
'Kodalith' Super Developer Powder
'Kodafix' Solution
Seriset sensitive emulsion (see note 2)
Wooden frame
Nylon or terylene mesh
Screen ink
Normal darkroom equipment, including Kodak Safelight Filter No. 1A

Notes
1. 'Line' film is a loose term applied to any high-contrast film intended for the reproduction of images consisting entirely of black and white, with no intermediate tones. Such films ('Kodalith' Films are an example) require a special high-contrast developer, such as 'Kodalith' Super Developer Powder. The 'line' film so termed by Mr Gresswell is a cheap non-branded variety.

2. Made by Screen Process Supplies Ltd, 24 Parsons Green Lane, London, S.W.6.

5.1.3 Blueprint material
This is known by various names: ferro-prussiate paper, plan copying paper, iron-printing process paper. The action of light is to change a soluble complex of yellow-brown ferric ferricyanide to an insoluble Prussian blue. Blueprint papers were first produced by Sir John Herschel, about 1842.

The material is easily made and the development and fixing is simply done by washing first in running water until the 'whites' are no longer yellow, then soaking in one percent hydrochloric acid solution, and finally washing again in running water.

Simple solutions:

Potassium ferricyanide	10 g
Distilled water	100 ml
Ammonium ferric citrate (green not brown)	25 g
or Ammonium ferric citrate (brown not green)	14 g
Distilled water	100 ml

Mix (in dark room or subdued light) equal volumes and brush on to thick semi-absorbent (duplicating) paper. Dry and keep in dark. The paper when fresh should be a yellow-brown and in daylight turns a bronze-blue.
(A test for freshness of the paper is to wash it under the tap: all the colour should wash away leaving the paper white.)

Solutions to produce a more rapid paper:

a. Ammonium ferric citrate (brown)	16 g/100 ml	Use equal volumes of each solution
b. Potassium ferricyanide	8 g/100 ml	
c. Ammonium ferric oxalate	9 g/100 ml	
d. Sodium ferric oxalate	15 g/100 ml	

Mix the solutions in the dark, brush on to paper and dry. Neither the *mixed* solutions nor the paper will keep more than about a month. Solutions *a, b, c* and *d* by themselves are quite stable.

5.1.4 Gelatine/dichromate
This was the basis of the 'carbon process' for printing photographs. When paper coated with a mixture of carbon black and gelatine is sensitised by soaking in potassium (or ammonium) dichromate solution, the action of light is to render the exposed gelatine insoluble. The unchanged gelatine can be dissolved away by washing in warm water.

A similar process, employing albumen and fish glue, instead of gelatine, was used for the preparation of printing blocks for pictures in newspapers, books, etc. A visit to the local newspaper may be quite rewarding. Photo-silk-screen printing could be carried out by interested pupils, see section 5.1.2.

5.1.5 Colour dyes
The fading of dyed fabrics is of interest to all housewives. It might be a suitable investigation for anyone considering colours. It is worth noting that the dyes used in photographic colour prints and transparencies are subject to fading if left exposed to light.

5.1.6 Blueprint paper used in a camera
Dried blueprint paper cut into strips can be used in a camera provided that it can be held in place and that the lens can be open for about twelve hours. An old box camera is admirably suitable.

After exposing and 'developing' (washing) the blueprint paper, it will be seen that the image is upside down, and that if it is turned the right way up the image is then laterally reversed (left to right and right to left).

Try using contact printing paper in a camera. The paper will need quite long exposures. Try an hour to start with.

5.1.7 Photograms: photographs without a camera
This is a form of direct photography carried out by holding opaque objects in contact with sensitised material and then exposing the material to light. The

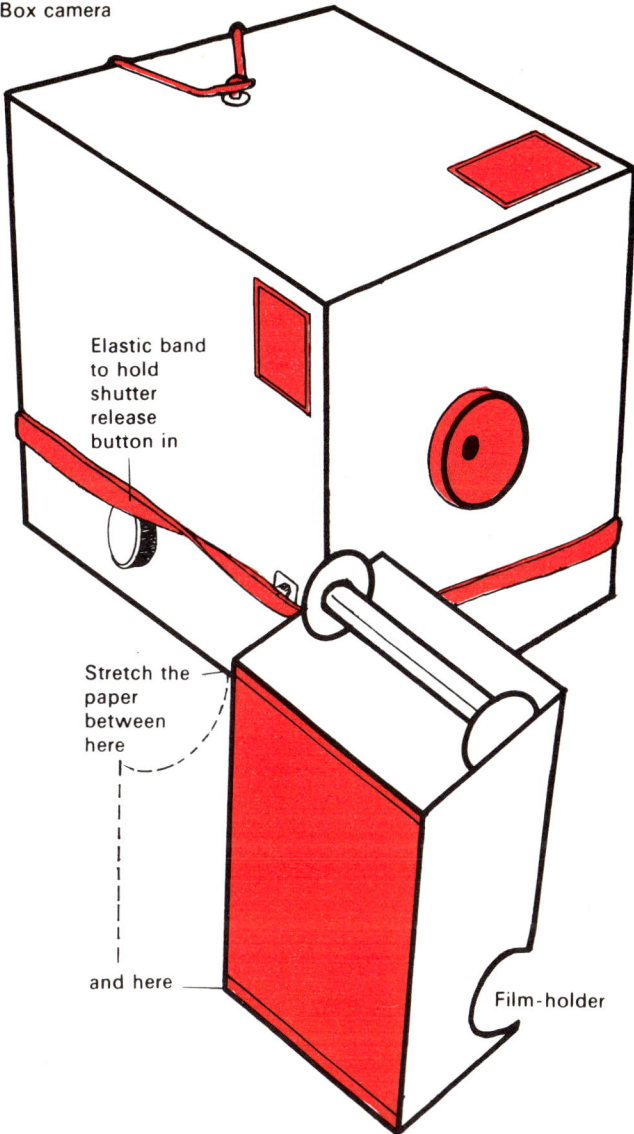

Box camera

simplest sensitised material is blueprint paper, which has the added advantage that it is only slowly changed so that the arrangement can be set up in shadow and then brought out into the full light without fogging the paper.

Put a sheet of blueprint paper face upwards on a newspaper and arrange a number of objects on it to make a pattern. Cover the paper and objects with a sheet of glass to hold them in contact with the paper. If sharp and clearly defined edges are required to the shadows then the objects must be in close contact with the paper, otherwise the edges are diffused.

Later, children can produce on blueprint paper photograms of $\frac{1}{8}$ in [3 mm] ball-bearings which model the structure of metals and show the formation of dislocations. This activity would help pupils to understand the particulate nature of matter, and could be introduced in either Combined Science or O-level science subjects. The method enables children to produce quite easily their own permanent records, something which is not so easily done with bubble rafts.

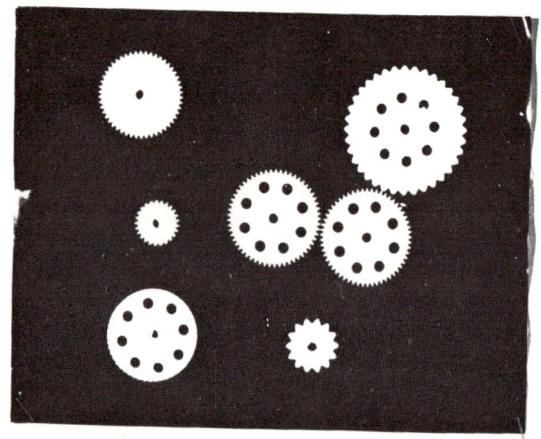

Cog Wheels.

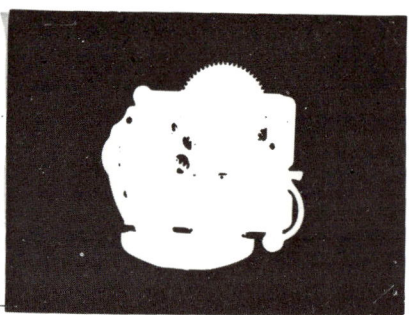

The inside of Timothy's clock.

The inside of Timothy's clock.

Inside a watch.

Cog Wheels.

Photograms for our TIME TOPIC.

Making Photograms.

Six people went into the dark room and I was one of them. Mr. Lane helped us. He showed us how to make photograms without a camera. First of all you have to close the door and put on a red light. Then Mr. Lane took out some photographic paper out of a box and put it on a base underneath a white light. Then he put the rest of the paper away. On one side of the paper is silky and the other side is not. Then an object is put on the silky side. The white light above is then turned on for about 20 seconds. After the light has been turned off the objects are tipped off. The paper then is put face down into a developer then it is turned over for a while, then it is put in a stop bath then it is put in a fixer. After that it is okay to open the door.

4th YEAR CUT OUT PHOTOGRAMS

NELSON

THE WAY OVER

QUEENBOROUGH CASTLE

← SHEPPEY

? →

Using ball-bearings to model atomic structure. This photograph shows the effect of dislocations in metals

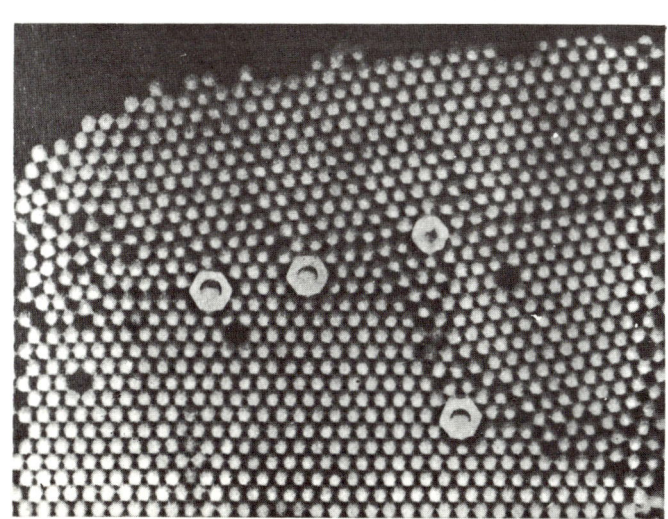

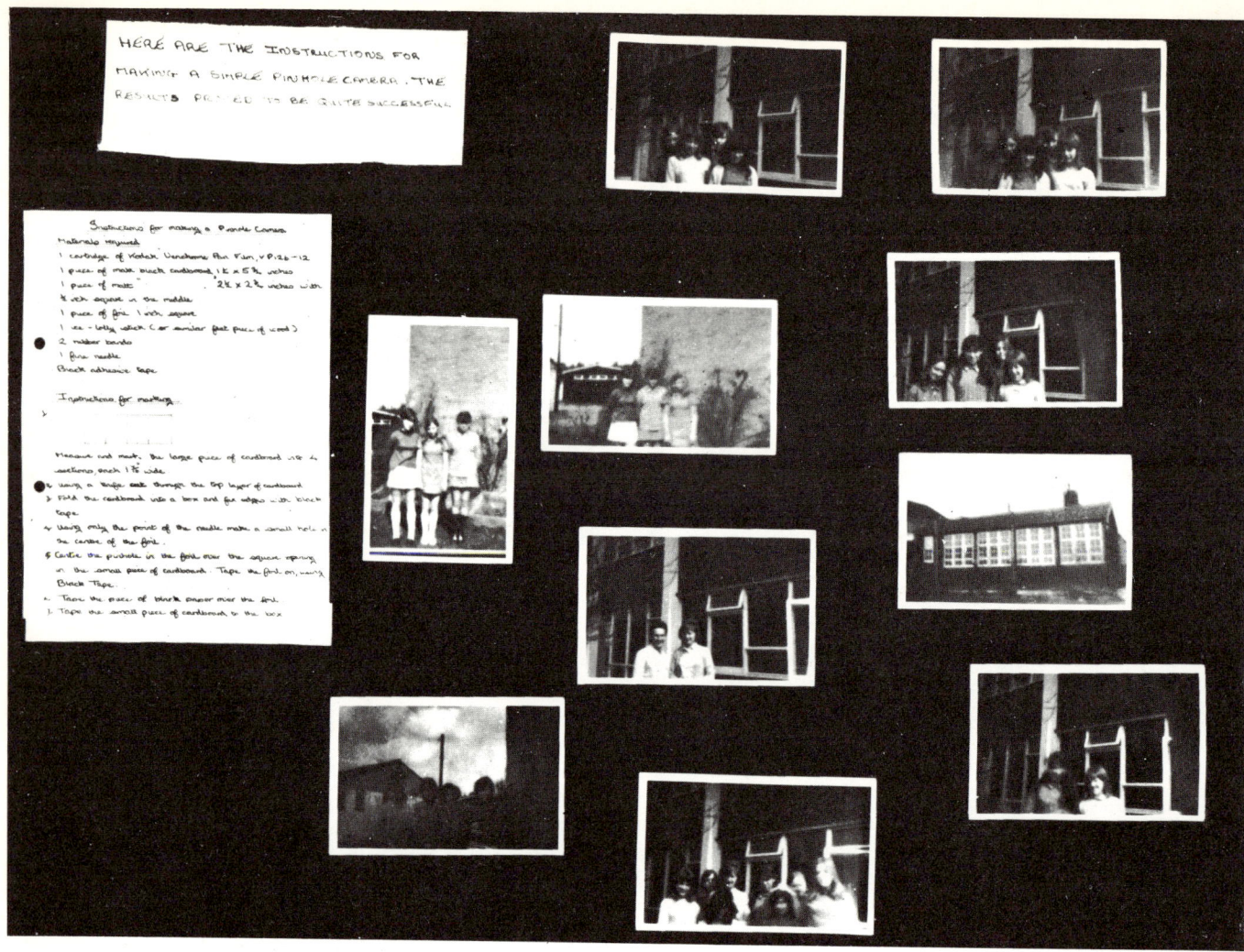

5.2 Making a pinhole camera

Many schools have constructed and used pinhole cameras, and have found that the difficulties encountered have been far less than had been imagined. One school reported that, provided all the materials were available, the average time of construction was about 1 hour 20 minutes.

The following instructions, reprinted by kind permission of Kodak Ltd, from *News for Education, Winter '70,* have been used as the basis for a number of work-cards, many of which have included improvements in the manufacture and use of the camera. A selection of hints from the present author is appended to this reproduced article.

A simply made pinhole camera

Making a pinhole camera is a good practical exercise for school children and provides a useful introduction to some basic principles in photography and optics. The design described here contains all the essential features of a camera, and has the added refinement of a film-winding device.

Materials required
1 cartridge of Kodak 'Verichrome' Pan Film, VP126-12
1 rectangular piece of matt black cardboard, $1\frac{1}{4} \times 5\frac{3}{4}$ in [32 × 147 mm]
1 rectangular piece of matt black cardboard, $1\frac{1}{2} \times 2\frac{3}{4}$ in [38 × 70 mm], with a $\frac{1}{2}$ in [12·5 mm] square hole in the centre
1 piece of aluminium foil, 1 in [25 mm] square
1 piece of black paper, 1 in [25 mm] square
1 ice-lolly stick or similar flat piece of wood
2 rubber bands
1 fine needle
black adhesive tape

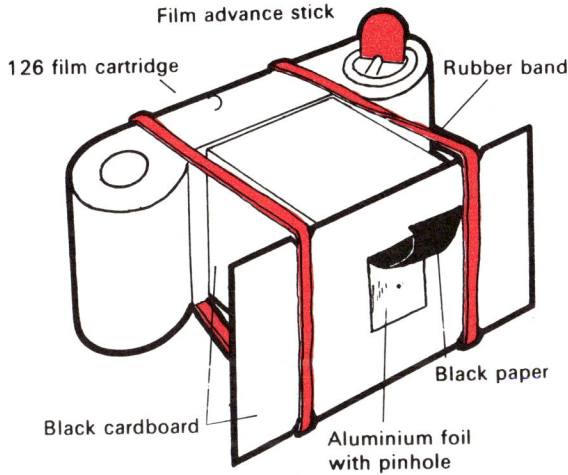

Making the camera
1. Measure and mark the large piece of black cardboard into four sections, each $1\frac{7}{16}$ in [36 mm] wide.

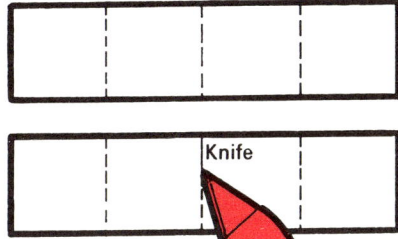

2. Using a knife, cut through the top layer of cardboard along each of the lines. This will make it easier to fold the cardboard.

3. Fold the cardboard into a box and fix the edges together with the black tape.

4. Using only the point of the needle, make a small hole in the centre of the aluminium foil.

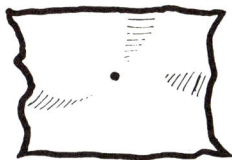

5. Centre the pinhole in the foil over the square opening in the small piece of cardboard. Tape the foil to the cardboard on all four edges.

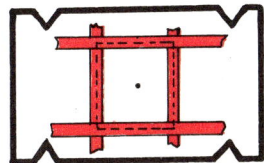

6. Put the small piece of black paper over the pinhole and tape it along the top edge.

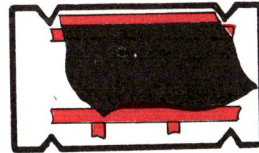

7. Tape the small piece of cardboard to the box. Make sure all the edges are taped tightly together so that no stray light can get into the camera.

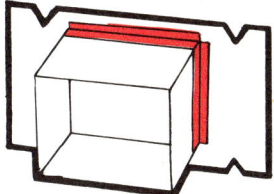

8. Push the camera box into the square opening in the film cartridge. This should be a tight fit so that no stray light can get into the camera.

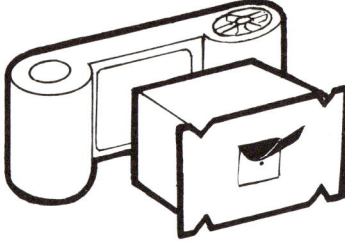

9. Use the two rubber bands to hold the camera box in place.

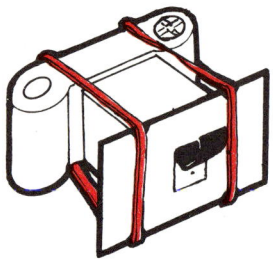

10. Trim the wooden stick so that it fits tightly into the round opening in the cartridge.

Winding the film
Turn the stick slowly and watch the yellow paper through the window in the cartridge. Count the figures as they pass the window and stop when the third and fourth figures 'one' are both showing. A picture can then be taken. Take all pictures with the third and fourth numbers of each set showing.

Taking the picture
Before taking a picture, make sure the camera is held perfectly still by taping it to a firm support. For pictures on sunny days, uncover the pinhole for about two seconds; on cloudy days, for eight seconds. Wind the film on immediately after taking each picture, making sure the pinhole remains covered between taking

Photographs taken with a cartridge pinhole camera

These pictures are reproduced by courtesy of Kodak Limited

pictures. After picture 12 has been taken, wind the film until all the yellow paper has passed the window. Then take the camera apart and have the film processed in the normal way.

Experimenting with the camera
It is interesting to compare the results obtained with different sizes of pinhole. Beginning with a coarse pinhole, the resolution at first improves as the hole size decreases and then rapidly deteriorates. The implications of this can be discussed. It is also useful to compare the results with those given by a lens camera, particularly with respect to depth of focus and evenness of field. (*End of Kodak article*).

Hints
a. Make sure that the cardboard is strong enough.

b. Use white cardboard and paint with *matt* black paint (obtainable from model shop or use blackboard paint) *after* construction.

c. Make sure that the camera is both light-tight and fits tightly into the film cartridge. Tape the camera to the cartridge.

d. Use cork borers to make a hole in the centre of the $1\frac{1}{2} \times 2\frac{3}{4}$ in [38 × 70 mm] rectangular piece of cardboard.

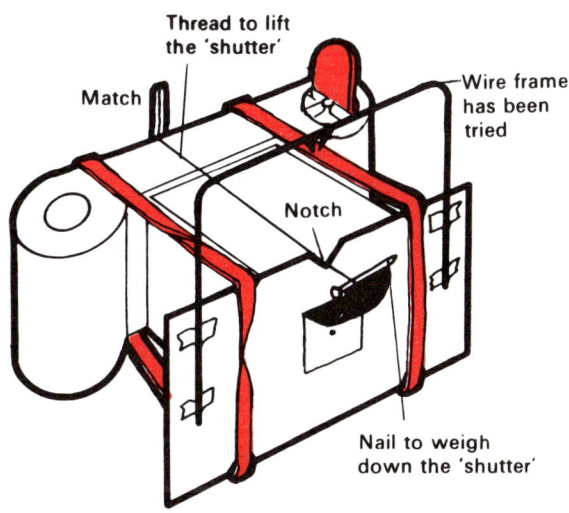

e. Glue a nail to the lower edge of the 'shutter' and lift the shutter by means of a cotton thread. When the cotton is released, the flap falls down and cuts off the light.

f. Make some form of viewfinder from thin wire or by putting a notch in the front cardboard and taping a match to the centre-back of the film cartridge.

g. Use elastic bands to fasten the camera to a flat piece of wood. This enables the camera to be placed on a firm surface without shaking. This is most important.

5.3 Working with a pinhole camera

Teacher's notes
a. This type of camera does not need focusing.

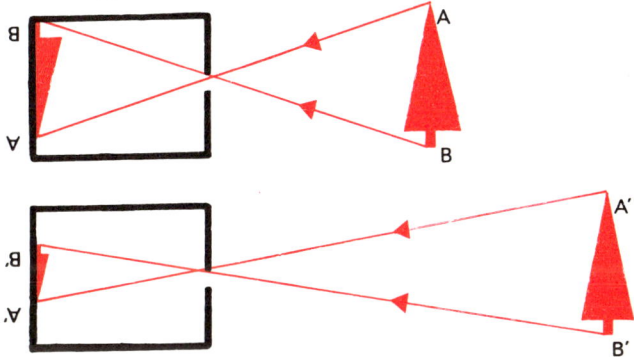

An object which is further away than another object remains in focus but gives a smaller image than the closer object.

b. The image is inverted.

c. Work with this camera needs to be parallel with work on developing and printing, otherwise the exposed film would have to be commercially developed and printed. A useful teacher's book is *Home Photography* by A. R. Pippard and K. MacDonnell, published by Johnsons of Hendon.

d. Aluminium foil is used to cover the hole in the cardboard in the front because the pinhole has to be a clean one. Fuzzy edges, made by pushing a pin or needle through paper or cardboard, would cause interference; a pinhole in aluminium foil can have a quite clean edge.

e. The work with a pinhole camera depends upon the knowledge, skill and resources of the child. It is possible either to develop a work-card system with simple steps based on:

Making the camera.

Using the camera.

Developing films.

Printing films (printing is probably easier for children than developing).

Work on associated themes.

Or, once the interest has been aroused channel it into a form of club or out-of-school activity.

Action of light on substances
For example, precipitate silver chloride using sodium chloride solution and M/10 silver nitrate solution. Filter the precipitate and expose the filter paper and the residue to sunlight. Try silver bromide and silver iodide. Use blueprint paper, see section 5.1.3.

Lenses
Make a simple telescope. Build your own lens camera, see *School Science Review*, vol 53, no 184 (1972), pages 615–18. Make a simple microprojector, see *School Science Review*, vol 52, no 181 (1971), pages 966–9.

5.4 Developing and printing

These are techniques the skills of which cannot be acquired just by reading books. If you are not able to develop and print photographs yourself, it is best to get someone to show you how it is done.

Reaction of three types of pupil to making a pinhole camera

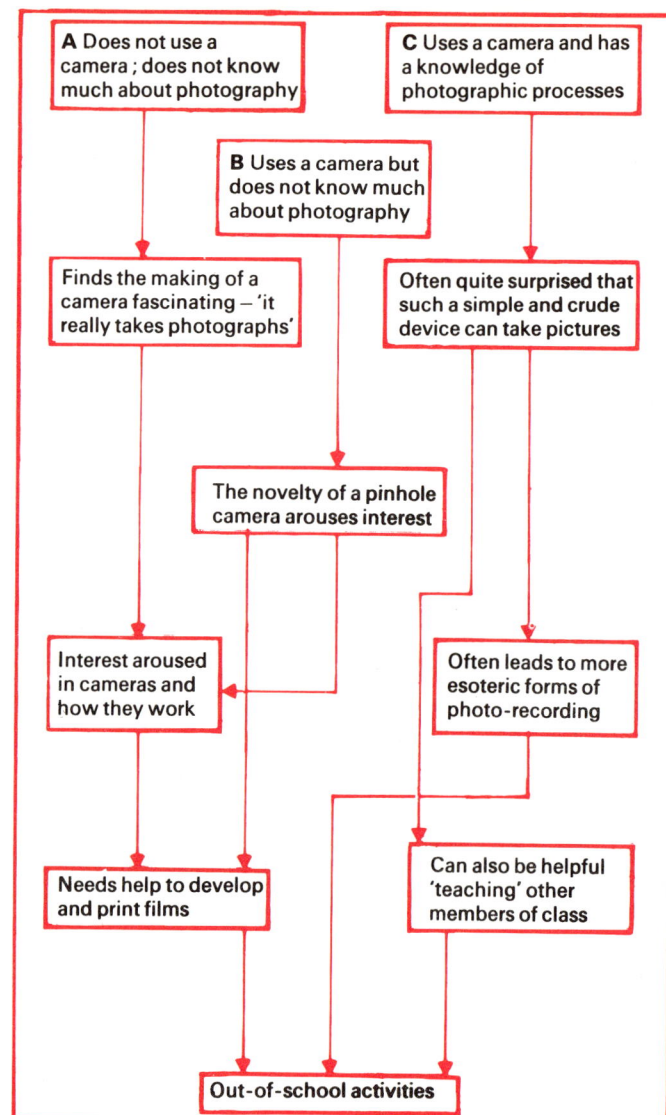

Are there any parents who would be prepared to help you or your class? Or any member of staff? Is there a local photographic society? Has a local Teachers' Centre the necessary facilities? Is there any likelihood of a course on photography—for example at the local technical college?

5.5 Simple equipment and materials

5.5.1 For developing a film (black and white)

a. Developing tank, eg Paterson's. Choose one to take the sizes of films you work with; the smallest Paterson tank takes 35 mm and 126 roll film only. The Universal Paterson tank can be adjusted for 35 mm, 126, 127, 120, or 220 roll films.

b. A measuring cylinder.

c. A beaker or jam jar, 500 ml capacity.

d. Thermometer, laboratory immersion type.

e. Stop clock or watch with second hand.

f. Clips to hang up film. Plastic clothes pegs are quite suitable. Make sure that there is a hole in the peg so that it can be hung from a hook or nail. Attach another peg to the bottom of the film to prevent it from curling up.

g. Developers can be made up, but a commercial concentrated developer, such as Unitol, is easy to dilute, keeps well and is generally convenient.

h. Fixers are either sodium or ammonium thiosulphate, commonly known as hypo. They also contain substances which make the solution weakly acidic so as to stop any further development of the film by the developer absorbed into the film gelatine base.

A convenient fixer which only needs diluting and can be used again and again (unlike a developer) is Redifix.

i. Liquid wetting agent to add to the last tankful of washing water. (Try a washing-up liquid—one drop may be sufficient.)

j. Distilled water. When the film is hanging up to drain and dry, pour some distilled water over it. This will remove the tap water, which contains dissolved solids and if allowed to dry on the film produces spots of deposit.

5.5.2 For printing a film

The easiest and simplest way of printing negatives is by contact printing. The process of printing is:

Exposure
Development—dish 1
Washing—dish 2
Fixing—dish 3
Washing
Drying

The minimum equipment is:

a. Printing frame, either bought or made.

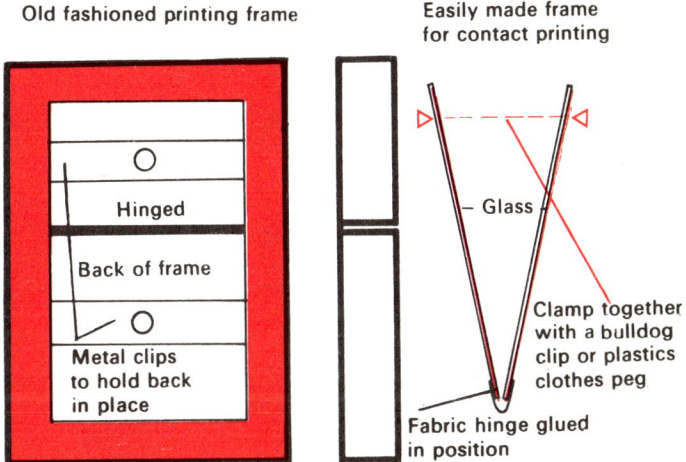

Old fashioned printing frame

Easily made frame for contact printing

b. Three dishes made of plastic or porcelain, in which to carry out developing or fixing.

c. Measuring cylinder.

d. Contact paper. There are many types and grades; it is advisable to get some advice before buying any.

e. A source of light.

f. A darkroom with 'safe' light.

If your school does not have a darkroom then a new contact paper may be of use. Kodak has produced contact paper C145 especially for schools. It is a paper of low sensitivity and can be handled safely in subdued artificial lighting. This paper can be developed in Kodak Universal Developer or in D163. It is available in packets containing 100 sheets of 89 x 127 mm [$3\frac{1}{2}$ x 5 in.].

g. Developer, eg Universal Developer, Con-sol, Developer 468.

5.5.3 Sources of information—black and white photography
Publications
'Make your own black and white slides', and 'A dark box for simple photographic printing', *School Science Review*, vol 52, no 180 (March 1971), pages 658–60 and 661–9.

Developing, Printing, Enlarging, Kodak Ltd.

Pippard, A. R., and MacDonnell, Kevin, *Home Photography*, Johnsons of Hendon. Gives useful information on developing and printing.

Time-Life Books, *The Life Library of Photography*, Time-Life International Ltd, New Bond Street, London W1E 8WE. This is a series of very useful books; details can be obtained from Time-Life International Ltd.

Film strips by Kodak Ltd
Developing and Printing, 41 frames.

Enlarging, 61 frames.

Chemistry of Photography, 47 frames.

All very useful and informative.

5.5.4 Sources of information—colour photography
Books
Starting with Colour, Kodak Ltd. Very basic technical information.
Let's take Colour Pictures Outdoors
Close-ups in Colour
Your Garden in Colour   } Useful for ideas and techniques.
Motor Sport in Colour
Sailing in Colour
Your Holiday in Colour

De Mare, Eric, *Colour Photography*, Penguin Books. Gives an outline of the principles and historical development of colour photography.

Film strips by Kodak Ltd
The Principles of Colour Photography, 37 frames. A comprehensive but fairly easily understood film. A strip lecture on the nature of light and colour, colour vision and the principles of colour photography.

ABC of Colour, 64 frames. Aimed at the beginner, this filmstrip gives hints and tips for obtaining technically perfect colour slides.

5.6 Use of a camera for recording

The users of cameras in school fall naturally and obviously into two groups: children and teacher.

For teachers the uses might be:

a. Recording class activities for Parent–Teacher Association lectures. Records of this nature are of particular use in promoting parent–teacher relationships as they can be employed to explain various aspects of science. These might be of interest to parents who are unfamiliar with newer forms of teaching: several explosive situations have been damped down by the presentation of lectures illustrated by photographs of 'real' children. In one school the science staff entertain the parents of the new entrants with a lecture showing the kind of work their children will be doing in and out of class. In this way the fears of some parents that 'teaching today is a lot of play' can be allayed before they even start. Furthermore, this approach often brings its own rewards with offers of help from the parents.

b. Teaching techniques. A good deal of assistance for children can be provided by a collection of pictures illustrating techniques and methods. These can be catalogued and stored and children encouraged to look up the reference when needed. Such a collection once started could be enlarged by a group of interested children who could be actors and cameramen.

Photographs could be in the form of slides or prints.

If slides are used then a small cheap projector is needed. The weekly magazine *Amateur Photographer* publishes once a year a guide to projectors which is worth consulting. (Try the local library for a copy.) The same magazine also publishes other guides, eg *Beginners' Camera Guide* and *Enlarger and Darkroom Guide.*

Another mode of recording is a cine camera. This is of particular use for photographing moving objects and processes. It is not of much use for static scenes, which are better recorded by a stills camera.

A word of warning. School loop projectors are often Standard 8, whereas most modern cine cameras are Super 8. The two are incompatible, which is a pity because a Standard 8 film can be cheaply made into a loop and then put into a cassette.

c. Work-card illustrations. Nothing brightens up a work-card like a photograph of familiar surroundings and a well-known school personality.

d. Our science needs to be a live subject, one which deals with things in everyday life. The laboratory processes need to be connected with industry, and visits to firms can—given permission—provide opportunities to photograph large-scale plant and processes.

e. Given a little encouragement, and a stock of films, children are avid camera users. The trouble is films are expensive. However, 35 mm bulk film can be purchased fairly cheaply (in August 1971, factory fresh FP4, HP4 was quoted at 50 ft for £1) and this can be wound into 35 mm cassettes using a bulk film loader, eg Watson 100. Suppliers can be found in the *Amateur Photographer.* Bulk film purchases and school laboratory developing and printing can dramatically reduce the cost per print.

Activities by children could include:

a. Personal records of the results of work done, eg photographs of models, experiments for notebooks.

b. Personal records of the apparatus seen or used. This would supplant free-hand drawings.

c. Class records for displays.

d. Illustrative work for projects, eg photographs of old steam engines and locomotives.

5.7 Useful apparatus for school use

The prices of photographic materials vary considerably from one supplier to another. Buyers would be well advised to consult the advertisements in the *Amateur Photographer* before making up their minds.

Camera
Very simple
Kodak Instamatic, Agfa Iso-Pak and Boots' Instapak are examples.

Simple 35mm
Exposure/aperture automatically selected, eg Dixon's Prinz Saturn 35 Auto (£27.95 in 1975). Cheaper cameras are available but the lens will not allow enlargements beyond enprint size.

Single-lens reflex 35mm
Built-in range-finder/focusing and light meter, eg Praktica LTL (£60 to £90 in 1975).

Bulk film loader 35mm
Watson 100 Cassette Loader from Marston and Heard Photographics Ltd, 378 Lea Bridge Road, Leyton, London E10.

Enlarger 35mm
There is a choice of models between £30 and £40.

5.8 Postscript

Photography is a subject of immense complexity; there are so many different aspects that something is bound to interest someone. Moreover, it is not confined to one branch of learning, but cuts across our arbitrary boundaries of science and arts. However, it is the complexity which frightens the newcomers and to them we suggest that they enlist the help of the local photographic society, or someone who has enough knowledge to explain the practicalities of the subject. It is the practical work which needs demonstrating, theory can be read up. Perhaps the local Teachers' Centre could help to arrange practical courses. One thing is certain, once a photographic society has been formed in

a school it can soon become self-perpetuating. Older members train newcomers very effectively so that they rapidly learn to keep the place neat and tidy!

It takes courage and determination for a tyro to start a class looking at science from the viewpoint of a photographer. It is not easy to get to a place where the path ahead can be seen, but once the journey is started there are plenty of pleasant byways to be explored.

Kodak Ltd produce a teaching kit, 'Fundamentals of Photography', which can be used both in science and art courses. Details can be obtained by writing to:

Kodak Ltd, 106H Education Service, Victoria Road, Ruislip, Middlesex.

6 Electrical toys

6.1 Low-voltage toys and safety

Experiment only with those toys which use low-voltage direct current, usually battery fed. If the current is supplied by a mains unit, make sure that the case is connected to earth on the plug. The green/yellow wire of modern apparatus, or the green wire of older apparatus, should be connected to the earthing pin of the mains plug; the other end of the earth wire should be joined to all exposed metal parts. Ensure that all mains units that you use are pronounced safe by the local education authority or by a qualified electrician, and that they incorporate reputable isolation transformers.

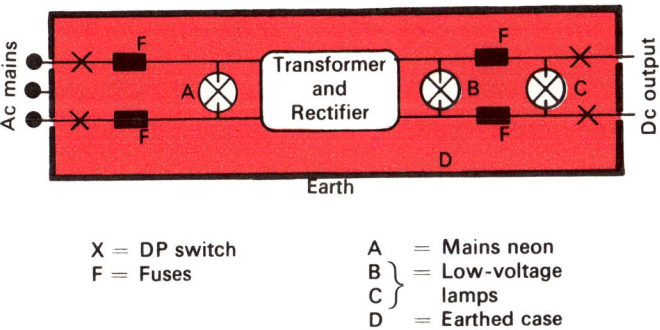

X = DP switch
F = Fuses
A = Mains neon
B } = Low-voltage
C }   lamps
D = Earthed case

As well as efficient earthing, both current-carrying leads should contain fuses, and both switches ought to be of double-pole type, so that on breaking the circuit the toy or apparatus is completely isolated from the mains unit. On the mains side there should be fuses and a double-pole switch, so that when the switch is off the mains unit is completely isolated from the mains. Lamps of the correct voltage at A, B and C (see circuit diagram) would indicate whether the unit is working.

A unit, stoutly made along these lines with screening so that it is impossible to touch wires at mains voltages, might be expensive but it it would be safe. The fuses on the output side are those likely to blow and could be replaced by overload switches.* These 'pop out' when there is an overload and can be reset when the overload or short is cleared. They are more expensive to start with, but pay for themselves in convenience and time saved. Another method of achieving the same result is to use a transistorised circuit using a feedback loop to prevent the unit being overloaded. Some commercial units employ this principle, and it is impossible to exceed a set current even if the output of the unit is short-circuited.

6.2 Electricity and safety

In view of the need for care in the use of mains units, some teachers may confine the work of junior forms to that involving batteries or accumulators, until the whole question of electrical safety can be explored during a class discussion. This could arise out of some 'happening'. For example, it would be useful to obtain examples of burnt-out equipment to form a 'Black Museum'.

Deaths and injuries due to electrical faults are only too frequent. The safe use of electricity for toys might well be the start of a study of electrical safety in everyday life. Think of high-tension electrical feeder lines on pylons and children flying kites; overhead electrical supply wires to some houses; railway electrical supplies by

*'Labpack' uses overload switches which can be reset when the short is cleared.

third rail or overhead wires; unshuttered three-pin plug sockets. (Even the shuttered type can be tripped with a match stick!)

In matters concerning electricity and safety a good guide is *Safety at School* (Educational Pamphlet no. 53, HMSO). The section on 'Electricity' in the chapter 'Safety in Science Laboratories' is particularly apposite.

6.3 How do we start and what do we do?

As with so many other situations, we start with something which interests the child. The question 'How does it work?' will produce an answer which might reveal certain inadequacies. Gentle probing will then help to spotlight an area of potential investigation which might be surprisingly elementary. Sixth-form pupils have been met who could recite Fleming's rule but could not connect accumulators in series/parallel to run a motor.

It is quite probable that many children will need to carry out simple investigations based on Stage 1 and 2 work (see Science from toys Stages 1 and 2) *before dealing with the more complex work of Stage 3.*
It might be worth sorting out the ideas we expect children to have at this stage. This does not mean we are suggesting a syllabus, but rather a check-list arranged in an order so that the items lower in the list depend to a certain extent on those which come before them. Thus the coupling of an electric motor via a switch to a battery depends upon a knowledge of:

a. The use of a battery and the idea of a closed circuit.

b. Which substances will conduct electricity—insulators, insulated wire, clean and dirty contacts.

c. The use of a switch—the switch *breaks* the circuit *not short-circuiting* the battery. (Children often find that short-circuiting the battery will stop the bulb or motor working.)

d. The number of batteries to use—this involves an elementary appreciation of voltage.

e. How to connect batteries in series and in parallel.

f. The need to try connecting leads from the battery so that the motor rotates in the desired direction.

6.4 The use of electrical toys

As with so many other toys, the work falls into two categories:

a. Working with the toy itself.

b Pursuing lines which are indicated by or associated with the toy. The table on the opposite page provides some ideas on these two lines of working.

6.5 Notes on apparatus, toys and methods employed

6.5.1 Shunting wagons
Some idea of the speeds before and after collisions are needed. It is not necessary to measure absolute speeds, eg in cm/s (centimetres per second), but they could be in any convenient unit. For example, if the wagons were illuminated by a flashing light and a long exposure photograph taken, then the movement of the wagon between flashes could be measured and the speed expressed as so many centimetres per flash. Details of

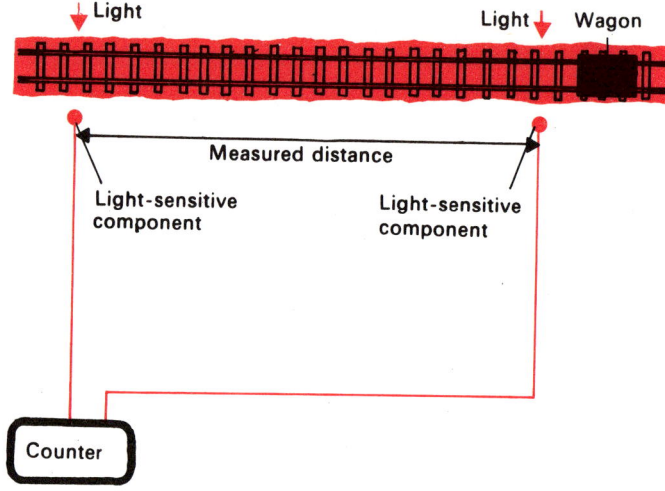

52

Toy	Working with the toy	Ideas/problems/investigations associated with or arising from the toy
Electric boat	1. Investigations into it as a boat—see Chapter 2. 2. Making a model boat and fitting it with a motor, etc. 3. How does the speed of the boat vary with the battery voltage?	1. How does it work? 2. Batteries and cells: which are best value for money? What is an accumulator? See *Change Stage 3* for details for making a small accumulator. This could be made and used to power a boat so that the study and making of an accumulator becomes relevant to a child. It is not just an academic exercise. 3. Mechanical systems, gearing and friction. 4. Energy changes. 5. Variables: what are the variables involved if we wish to increase the speed of the boat? 6. Why does the battery run down so quickly? Work on: (*a*) capacity, (*b*) current taken by different motors and (*c*) available mechanical energy of different motors. 7. Ideas about horse-power and work-units. 8. Electric motor—can we make a simple one? How does it work?
Slot racing cars and railways	1. See *Science from toys Stages 1 and 2*. 2. Shunting wagons and work on momentum. 3. Climbing slopes. How is the gradient of a slope measured? 4. Energy conversions. 5. Need for banking track on curves. How does it vary with different curves? How is a curve measured? Why do trains tend to leave the rails on curves? 6. Prepare a 'schematic diagram' (if necessary of own devising) showing the track and controls and how the current flows.	1. Items 1–4 and 8 from electric boat. 2. What does the mains unit do? What is: Alternating current (ac)? Direct current (dc)? A rectifier? A transformer? A speed controller? Mains voltage? 3. If the system will not work, how is the fault traced? Preparation of a branching programme—check the efficiency of such a programme.
Electrical points and signals		1. How do they work? (see *Science from toys Stages 1 and 2*, section 10.12). 2. Electromagnets (see *Metals Stages 1 and 2*). Make a small electromagnet from copper wire and a 4 in [100 mm] nail. Vary the current through the coil and measure how many nails are picked up.

this method can be found in *Nuffield O-Level Physics: Guide to Experiments 4*.

The foregoing method uses a stroboscope. Could a flasher bulb, such as is used in some torches, work instead? Perhaps the bulb could be fitted to a truck and the electricity picked up from the rails.

For very able pupils, the speeds of wagons can be determined using a digital counter triggered by a photo-electrical switch.

Details of using a scaler as a timer can be found in *Nuffield O-Level Physics: Guide to Experiments 4*, page 12.

A simpler and very much cheaper method is given in section 6.5.2.

6.5.2 Simple timing unit
This involves four modules:

a. A clock which produces regular pulses of electricity.

b. A counter to count the pulses.

c. An *on* switch which allows the pulses to enter the counter.

d. An *off* switch which cuts off the pulses from the counter.

Both the *on* and *off* switches are cheap micro-switches operated by very small pushes.

The counter is an electromechanical one similar to that used to tot up telephone calls.

The clock is a well-known electronic circuit, very simple and easy to construct from discrete components. It could well be made using an integrated circuit, but these modern wonders, which compress into a single chip of silicon the complexities of a radio set, are a little off-putting unless you are familiar with them.

Such a timing unit could be used for timing:

a. Model cars and lorries.

b. The falling of a ball.

c. School sports events.

d. Balls rolling down slopes.

e. Boats being towed in a plastics gutter, see Chapter 2.

f. Electric boats in a plastics gutter, see section 6.4.

Electronic clock module—variable frequency A-stable multivibrator driving a relay

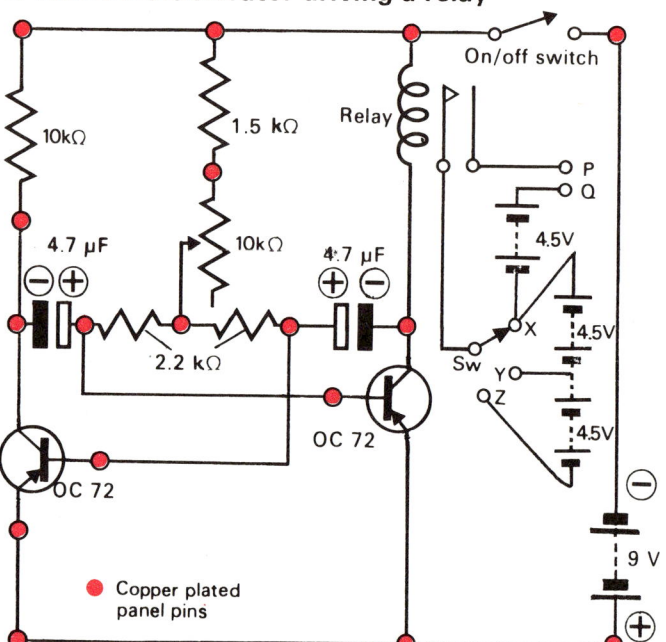

PQ are output terminals.

Sw is a rotary single-pole three-way switch to select different voltages from a battery made up of three 4·5 V flat batteries joined in series.

The relay is a simple make-when-energised type operating off 6 V.

Batteries: Three 4·5 V flat batteries; one 9 V radio battery.

Transistors: Two OC72.

Connections viewed from side:

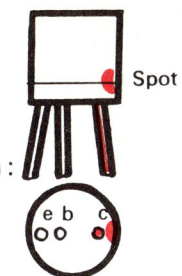
Spot

Connections viewed from underneath:

Alternative: Two BC477.

Connections viewed from underneath: cut off case connection.

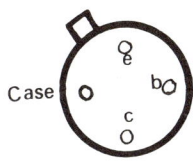

Capacitors: Two 4·7 µF electrolytics, maximum voltage 10–15 V.

Resistors:
One 1·5 kΩ ⎫
Two 2·2 kΩ ⎬ 0·125 W carbon film.
One 10 kΩ ⎭
One 10 kΩ potentiometer and knob (midget control, either log or linear track).

Relay: RS 6 V make and break; miniature open PC relay.

On/off switch.

Voltage selector switch: Single-pole, three-way switch and knob.

Output terminals: Two 4 mm sockets (one red, one black).

Cut a piece of five-ply, 200×100 mm [$7\frac{7}{8} \times 3\frac{15}{16}$ in], to act as a baseboard. Hammer copper-coated panel pins into the baseboard so that they are firm. Mount the controls and terminals on the panel. Fix the control panel to the baseboard and wire and solder the rest of the components into place.

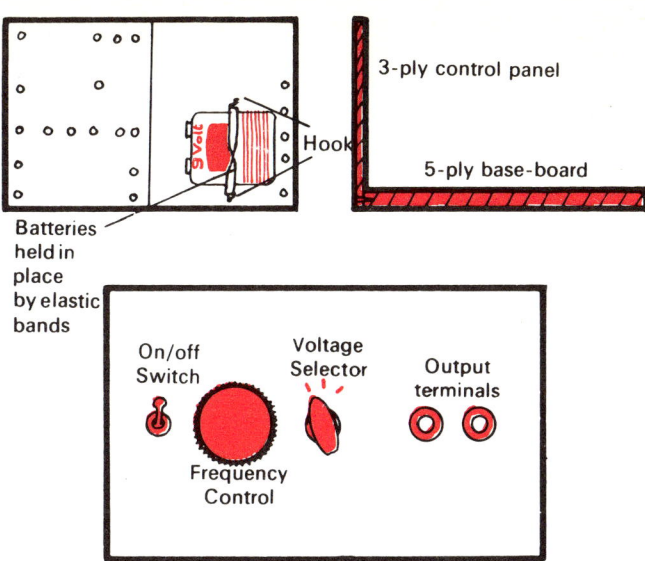

When it is switched on, the relay should click away. The frequency of the clicks can be altered by changing the setting of the 10 kΩ potentiometer.

Such an electronic clock can be used as a metronome, to flash a light bulb on and off, and to feed a counter unit.

Counting module
This device starts counting when the *on*-switch is momentarily triggered, and is cut off when the *off*-switch is triggered. The whole set-up is:

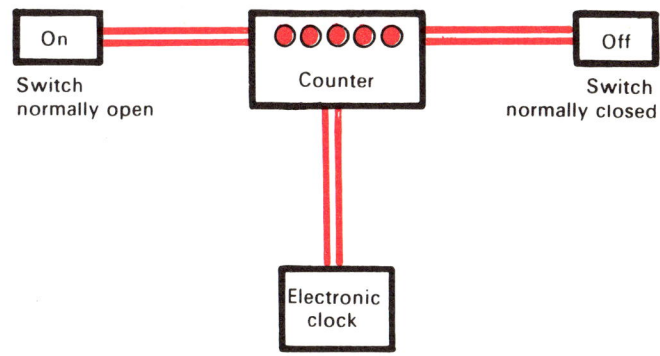

As the *on*-switch makes contact only momentarily, an arrangement known as a 'latching relay' is used. The momentary blip causes the latching relay to lock on until the *off*-switch interrupts the circuit and causes the relay to 'drop out'. While the latching relay is operating, the counter adds up the pulses received from the electronic clock.

The circuit is:

(circuit diagram with points P, Q, E, X, F, C, Y, A, D, B, 6 volt battery, R, S, U, T. Labels: Counter display; Normally closed T - To Off Switch; Normally open - To On Switch; Latching circuit shown in colour)

The relay is a 6 V two-pole change-over. (If only a 12 V relay is available then sufficient batteries must be used to make up 12 V.)

A and *B* are the tabs on the relay which are connected to its coil winding. *E, F, C, D* are the contact tabs which are used.

Note. Contacts *X* and *Y* are open until the relay is energised.

P, Q, R, S, T, U are 4 mm plugs.

P, Q are connected to the clock.

R, S to the *on*-switch.

T, U to the *off*-switch.

How it works
When *R* and *S* are connected by the *on*-switch, there is a momentary 'on' in the circuit *RABS*, and contacts *X* and *Y* are closed because the relay coil is energised. This switches on the latching circuit *ACDUTSBA* because the contacts at *Y* are closed; the *on*-switch can drop out, but the latching circuit is still complete until the *off*-switch, when tripped, breaks the circuit. Contacts *X* and *Y* are then opened, the latching circuit is broken, and the circuit from the clock to counter is also broken because the contacts at *X* are opened.

Construction
The counter is a 6 or 12 V electromechanical counter. Such counters are advertised in the columns of radio and electronic magazines. The prototype counter was capable of counting up to at least 21 pulses/s although it was advertised for only 10 pulses/s.

The relay is a 6 V, two pole change-over type.

The sockets are standard 4 mm red/black.

On and off switches
These are micro-switches from RS Components Ltd.

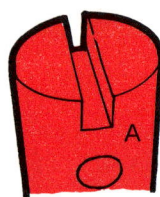

A is a small knob with a slit in the top and a hole through the shaft; it will turn slightly in either direction with a very small force.

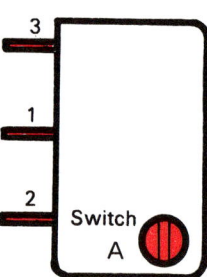

On the side of the switch are three metal tabs labelled 1, 2, 3. At rest, the switch joins 1 and 2; when the switch is operated, the contact between 1 and 2 is broken and 1 is joined to 3.

The *on*-switch uses contacts 1 and 3 and is normally open; the *off*-switch uses contacts 1 and 2 and is normally closed. The switches are mounted on small baseboards and connected to 4 mm sockets.

The shaft of the switch can be rotated by a length of thin copper wire if it is threaded through the hole and bent over so that one end fits snugly in the slot.

The wire acts as a lever, and a slight force applied to the end of the wire is sufficient to actuate the switch.

Connecting leads
The leads to the *on* and *off*-switches should be long enough to allow the object to be timed over the maximum distance available. They should be fitted with banana plugs to fit the 4 mm sockets. The counter and clock can be close together and connected by short leads.

6.5.3 Making a simple dc electric motor
Commutator

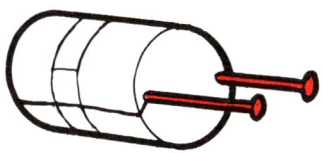

The advantages of using the type of commutator illustrated here are:

It is easy to make.

The small brads clean themselves and the copper wire

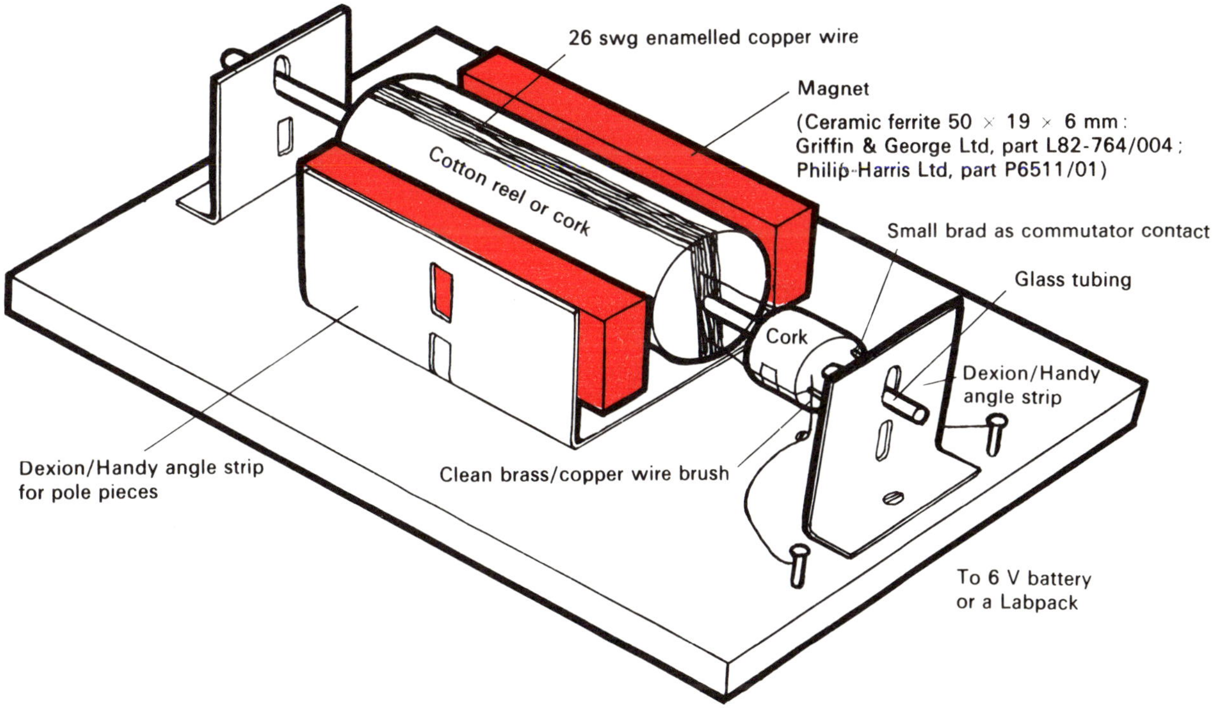

brushes during the rotation of the commutator.

The position of the commutator can be adjusted by rotating the cork to get the best results.

Armature
Make from a cotton reel or cork with 200–300 turns of wire wound on.

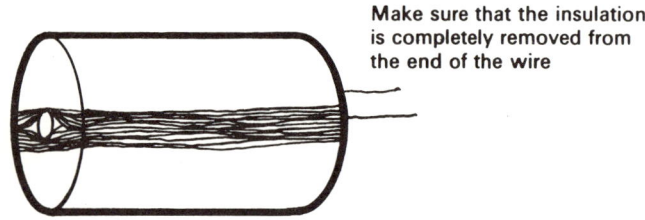

Make sure that the insulation is completely removed from the end of the wire

No measurements are given throughout because these depend on the size of the cotton reel.

Pole pieces
Made from Dexion/Handy Angle strip bent into the shape shown.

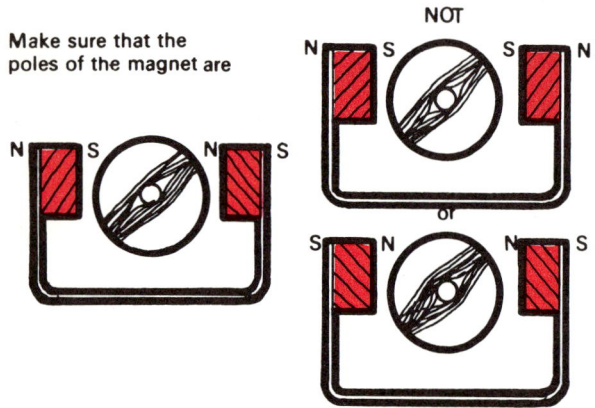

Make sure that the poles of the magnet are

The size will depend upon the diameter of the cotton reel with the wire wound on it.

6.5.4 Example of a branching programme for fault-finding
This is an example of systematic working. Some people automatically erect a programme like this for problem-solving and carry out the investigations and trouble-shooting almost instinctively. More work blindly, trying first one expedient and then another; it is often more by luck than judgement that they arrive at a satisfactory conclusion.

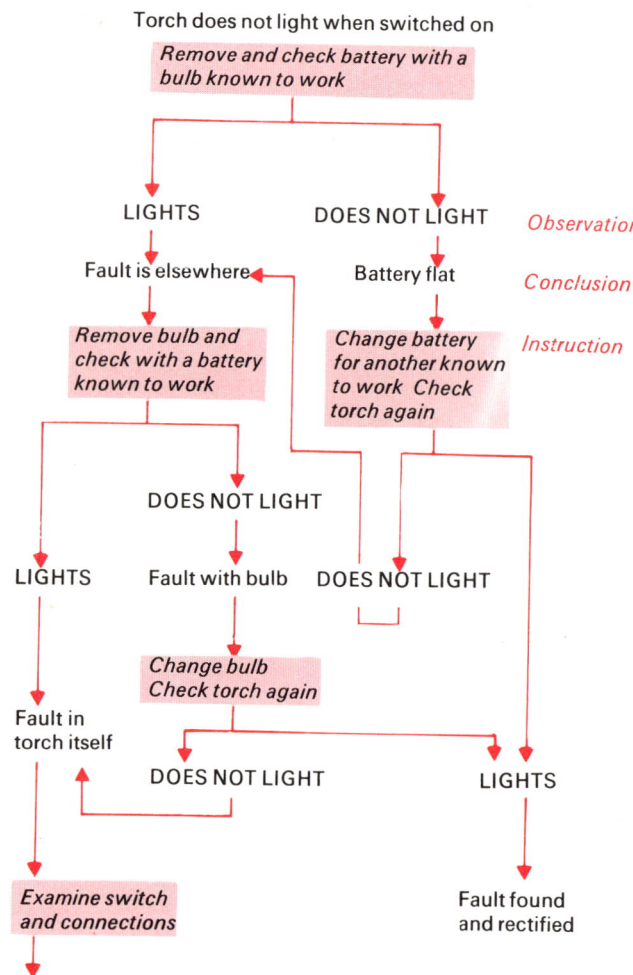

The diagram above shows the *observation,* the conclusion to be drawn and the *instruction.*

Such a programme is using ideas which are basic to computer techniques, for example the response which is looked for is either *light* or *no light*. This is the same as *go* or *no go*, which in the binary code becomes 1 or 0 (1 v 0).

6.6 Radio control of models

This can be a highly complicated business. It can be a very dangerous hobby for anyone who is ham-fisted or does not know what he is doing. It is essential to know that, for example, a 2 m wingspan model weighing some 3 kg and, powered by a 60 motor (0·60 cubic inch capacity), flies at speeds of 80 mile/h [128 km/h] and can easily attain 150 mile/h [241 km/h] in a power dive. Such a missile in the wrong hands is lethal. On the other hand, slow-flying models are perfectly safe under all normal circumstances, given that reasonable precautions are taken.

Radio control can be used with model motor boats, yachts and racing cars.

Making a radio-controlled model could well be a joint venture between the craft and science departments, as it involves working with wood and metal (and perhaps plastics), and learning about and constructing electrical and radio circuits. It is a project which would keep a team of enthusiasts absorbed for quite a time without their becoming bored.

6.7 Sources of supply

Radio, electrical and electronic components
The following postal suppliers issue catalogues:

BiPak, PO Box 6, Ware, Herts. List of semiconductors; data on the 74 series of integrated circuits.

J. Bull (Electrical) Ltd, 7 Park Street, Croydon CR0 1YD. Monthly bulletin; yearly catalogue.

Electrovalve, 28 St Jude's Road, Englefield Green, Egham, Surrey. *Handbook of Transistor Equivalents and Substitutes;* catalogue.

Henry's Radio Ltd, 303 Edgware Road, London W2. Catalogue.

Home Radio (Components) Ltd, 234–240 London Road, Mitcham CR4 3HD. Catalogue.

The Radio Shop, 16 Cherry Lane, Bristol BS1 3NG. Catalogue.

RS Components Ltd, PO Box 427, 13–17 Epworth Street, London EC2. Catalogue.

G. W. Smith & Co. (Radio) Ltd, 11–12 Paddington Green, London W2. Catalogue.

Most firms make a small charge for their catalogues.

Hot Wheels: toy shops, Woolworths.

Publications
Monthly magazines
Aero Modeller.
Practical Electronics.
Everyday Electronics.
Radio Modeller.
Radio Control Models and Electronics.
Wireless World.
Practical Radio.
Radio Constructor.

Books
Warring, R. H., *Single Channel Radio Control,* MAP Ltd.*
Warring, R. H., *Multi Channel Radio Control,* MAP Ltd.
Siposs, George, *Model Car Racing by Radio Control,* MAP Ltd.
Connolly, Phillip, and Smeed, Vic, *Radio Control, Model Boats,* MAP Ltd.
Introduction to Single Channel R/C Aircraft, Singlet Set, Low Cost Proportional, The Propo Book, Theory and Practice of Model Radio Control. From Radio Modeller's Book Division, 64 Wellington Road, Hampton Hill, Middlesex.

*Model and Allied Publications Ltd, 13–35 Bridge Street, Hemel Hempstead, Hertfordshire.

7 Trains and cars

Here we have the delight of nearly all boys and quite a few girls. Of all toys these should be winners, from the simple push-along car for the infant to the sophisticated radio-controlled racer costing £200 a time; they interest children of all ages and abilities. They can be starters for many different branches of study, and the same toy can be used time and time again to spark off work at varying levels within the same class. To one child it provides the opportunity for the study of electricity, for another there are problems of energy, and for yet another there is the very real problem of putting the track together and coupling the electrical links.

Some of the problems of electrical circuits have been dealt with in Stages 1 and 2 but there are still many questions which have not yet been asked.

7.1 Gears*

Many model cars and trains have some form of gearing. What do gears do? Why have them? Do you get something for nothing if you use gearing? Why does a full-size car have a gearbox?

The first thing to establish is that, generally, gears either speed something up or slow it down. They are also used to change the direction of drive.

Which way do the gears work on the toy? Does the motor run faster or slower than the driving wheels?

It would be a help to have sufficient Meccano parts to make up simple gear systems and to make this section the subject of a work-card. It is suggested that it would be more helpful if children made up the gearing systems rather than have models already put together. Perhaps a framework to house the gears could be constructed from Meccano parts, and then screwed down on a wooden baseboard. Sufficient gears, collars, handles and axle rods could be kept in a labelled box. (Don't forget to have a list of the contents on the lid.)

This framework could be kept screwed on a base-board

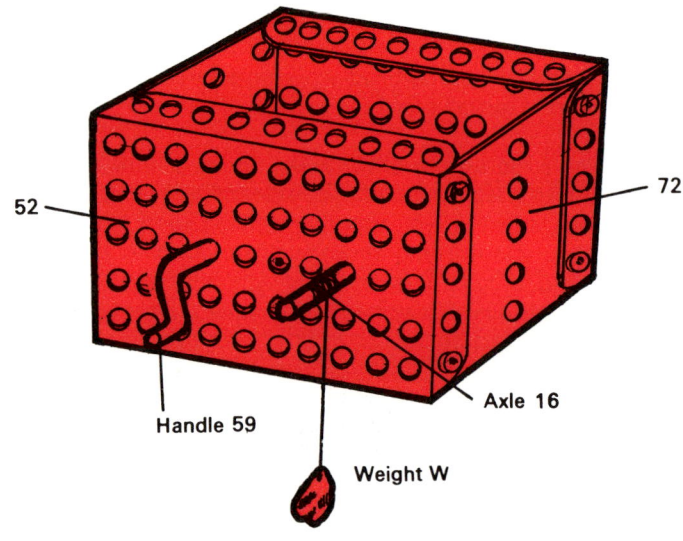

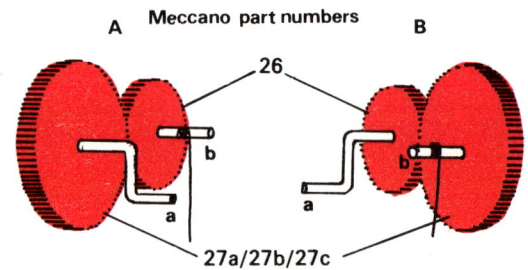

Meccano part numbers

*See Change Stage 3, section 3.3.11.

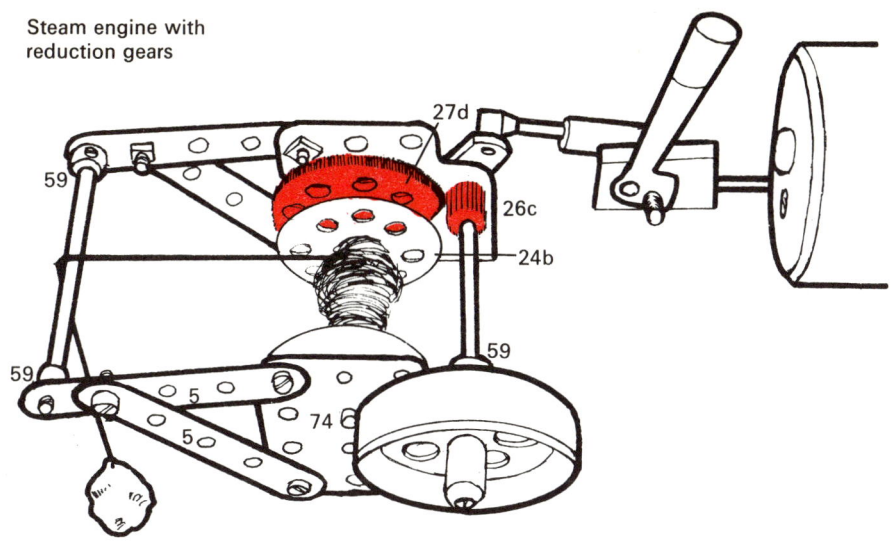

Steam engine with reduction gears

Meccano part numbers

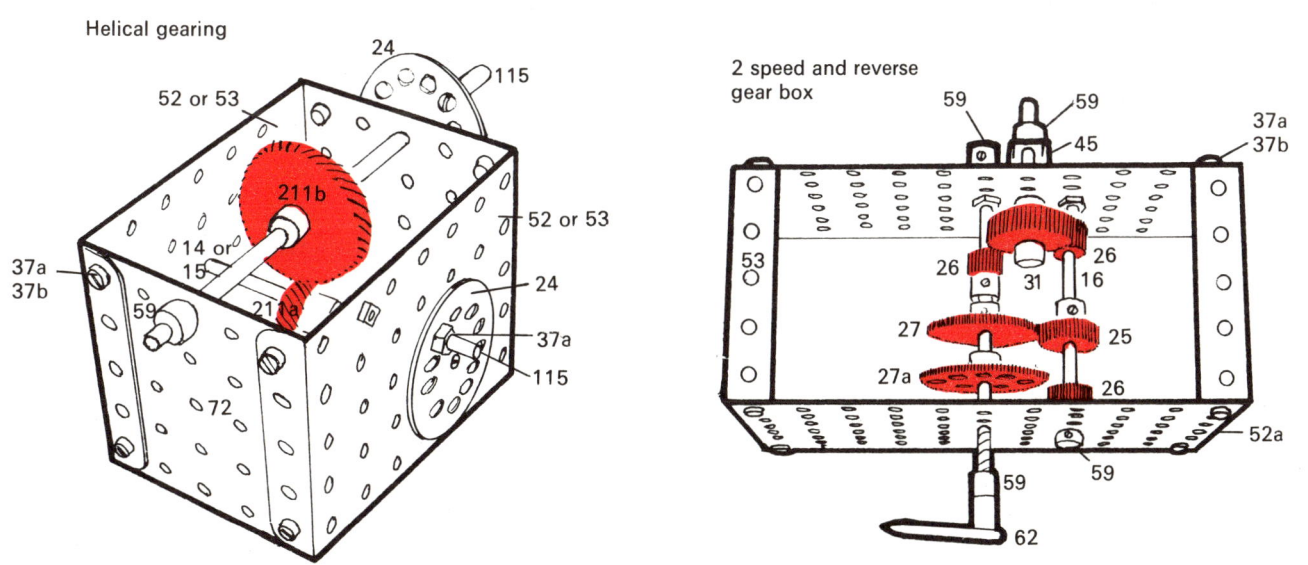

Helical gearing

2 speed and reverse gear box

61

Drive the axle by a gear train and see the advantages and disadvantages of using system A or B to wind up the weight W.

If the handle is turned once, how many times does the axle rotate? Try it with the systems A and B. Suppose the number of turns the handle makes is T_{handle} and the number the axle makes is T_{axle}. Is there any relationship between the ratio

$$\frac{T_{handle}}{T_{axle}}$$

and the ratio

$$\frac{\text{Number of teeth on handle gear-wheel}}{\text{Number of teeth on axle gear-wheel}}$$

Try different gear ratios.

Sometimes gearing is used to change the direction of drive as shown below.

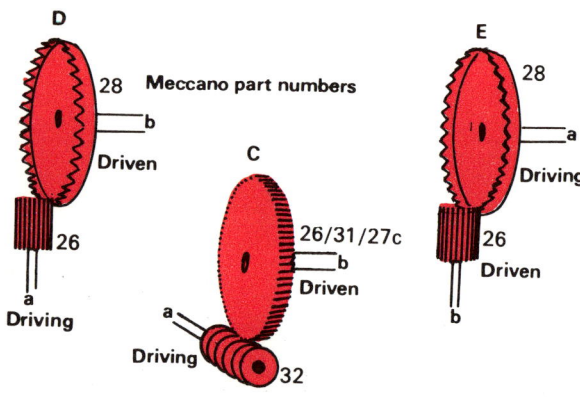

Worm-wheel drives and contrate gearing both transmit the drive through a right angle.

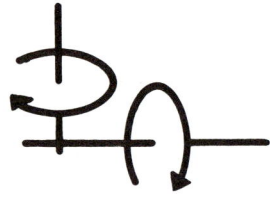

Note the difference in speeds between the *a* and *b* shafts in the worm-wheel gearing. What other outstanding difference is there between this gearing and the others which have been tried?

Once again use Meccano parts to investigate the gearing. Some form of concise recording is needed. Perhaps something like the following table could be devised.

Which of these gearings is used in the back axle of a car? Which of these gearings would you use in a crane to enable you to lift heavy loads? Explain why.

7.2 Gears and a car

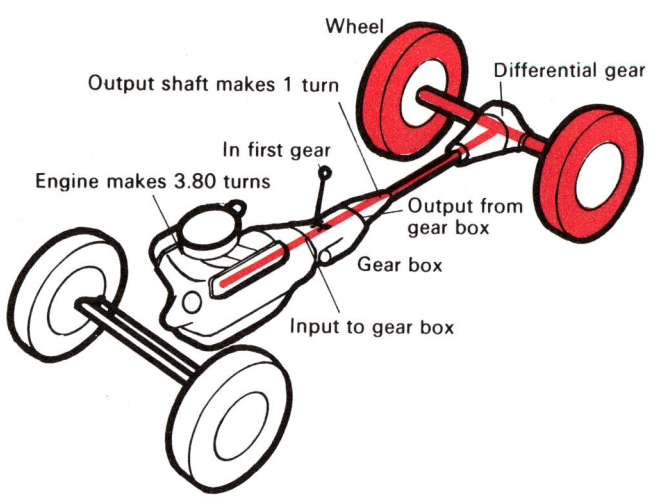

Gearing data of a familiar car

	Number of turns of input to gearbox	Number of turns of output from gearbox
Top gear	1·00	1
Third gear	1·41	1
Second gear	2·18	1
First gear	3·80	1

Summary of information about gearing

Type of gearing	Rough sketch: *a* is the driving gear *b* is the driven gear	Number of turns *b* makes for one turn of *a*, $=T_b$	Number of teeth on *a* $=N_a$	Number of teeth on *b* $=N_b$	Ratio N_a/N_b	Is the gear reversible? ie can it be driven by *b*?	Any other information
Simple 'speed-up' gear A	(a)(b)	2	20	10	$\frac{20}{10}=2$	Yes	The ratio N_a/N_b is the same as the ratio T_b/T_a
Simple 'slow-down' gear B							
Contrate gearing 'slow-down' D							
Contrate gearing 'speed-up' E							
Worm-drive gearing C			If *a* is given one turn how much does *b* turn?				

In top gear, the output shaft from the gearbox turns once for every revolution of the engine. In first gear, the engine has to turn 3·80 times for one revolution of the output shaft.

Questions such as the following soon indicate if pupils have an *understanding* of the concepts associated with gearing.

If the mile/h [km/h] in top gear for 1000 rev/min of the engine is 15·6 [25] what is the speed in mile/h [km/h] for 1000 rev/min in third, second and first gears? If the 'running in' speed for a new car is 45 mile/h [72 km/h], what are the comparable speeds in the other gears?

If the maximum rev/min is 6400, what are the comparable maximum speeds in the gears?

Data such as these can be obtained from car-makers' catalogues or from magazines such as *Motor* or *Autocar*.

7.3 Other gears in everyday life

Bicycle
For one turn of the large cogwheel, how many turns does the back wheel make?

For one turn of the back wheel, how many turns does the large cogwheel make?

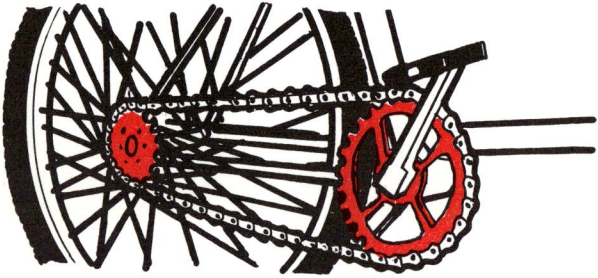

Is the gearing on a bicycle a 'speed-up' or a 'slow-down' gear?

Why do you think this type of gearing has been adopted?

Number of turns of the large cogwheel (input)	Number of turns of the back wheel (output)
1	

Wood/metal drill
What kind of gear system is this?

How many times does the drill bit (output) turn for one revolution of the large cogwheel (input)?

Other apparatus containing gears:

Lawn mower　　Record player　　Food mixer
Egg beater　　Watch/clock　　Some toys
TV/radio/tape　　Typewriter　　Some cameras
　recorder　　Sewing　　Telephone dialling
Electric drill　　　machine　　　mechanism

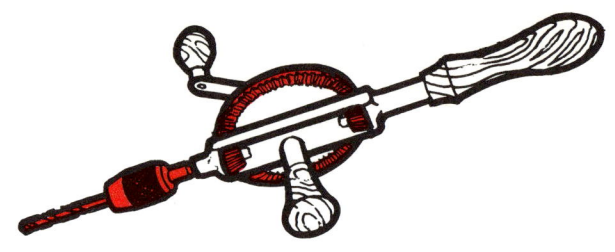

7.4 Engineless cars

7.4.1 Ideas which might develop
How many juniors race toy cars down slopes? Such toys can be used to widen a child's experiences of energy and movement.

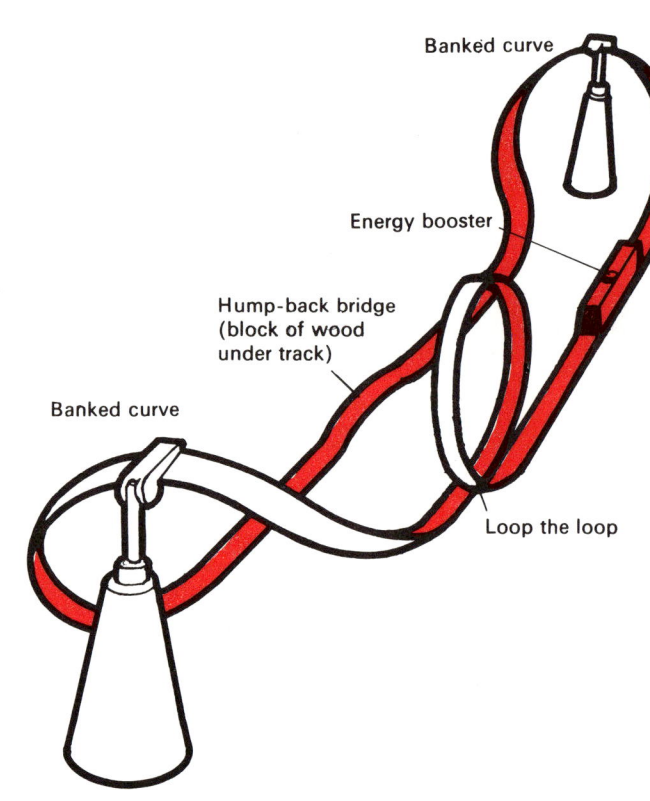

Questions

Where does energy come from?

Why doesn't the car fall from the inside of the loop?

What is the biggest diameter loop the car will go round and still remain on the track?

What happens if the curves aren't banked?

Why does the car leave the track as it passes over the hump-back bridge?

Why does the car slow down after passing over the bridge?

How can we calibrate the energy booster?

What effect does loading the car have on the speed?

Answers and ideas

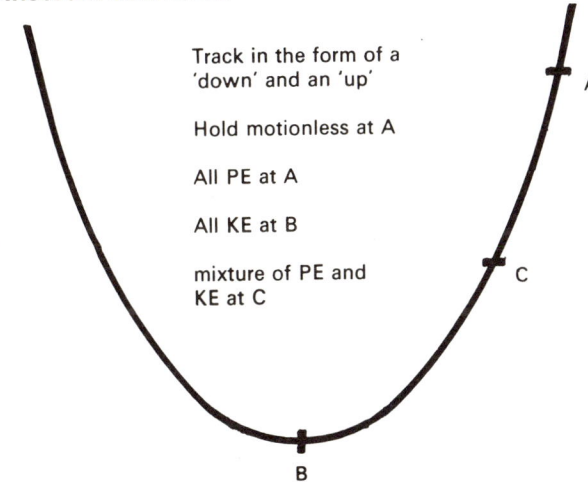

Track in the form of a 'down' and an 'up'

Hold motionless at A

All PE at A

All KE at B

mixture of PE and KE at C

Moving objects have energy.

Moving bodies tend to keep moving straight on.

Friction tends to slow cars.

Friction cannot be reduced to nothing.

A body has potential/latent/stored energy because of its position.

When a car runs up and down a switchback its kinetic energy (KE) and potential energy (PE) are interchangeable.

An engineless car never ends up higher than the level it started from unless it has received a suitable form of energy. (You can't get something for nothing: energy has to be paid for in terms of other energy.)

Calibrating the booster:

Energy booster

Measure the vertical height to which a car will go.

Plot h against the booster number.

If the booster is kept on the same number how does h vary with the weight of the car?

7.4.2 A problem of hills and speeds

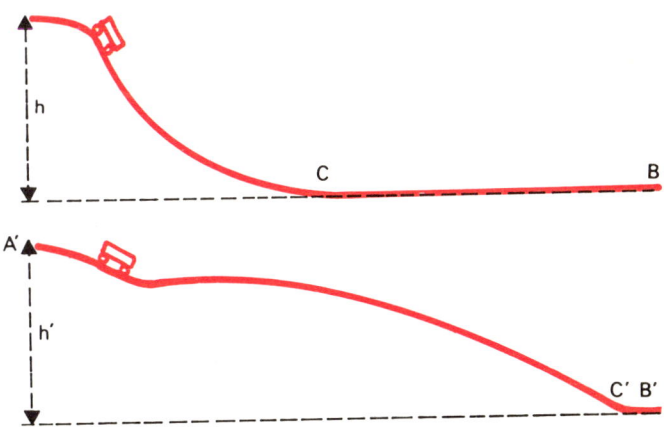

a. Use two Rocket tracks to form the switchbacks ACB and $A'C'B'$. In both cases, the height of drop should be the same, ie $h = h'$. Which one would you take if you were racing one car against another?

Race the cars down the tracks. Switch over the cars to make sure that one car hasn't undue frictional losses. Remember you are testing track slopes not comparing cars.

It might be worthwhile selecting two cars which, as far as possible, have identical losses. This can be done by running a number of cars down a plank and picking out two which go down together. This is harder than it sounds and will take some careful thought and planning.

Hold a discussion with children before they start their investigations. By so doing, some assessment could be made of their understanding of energy, and leading questions could be put to them to help them develop their ideas.

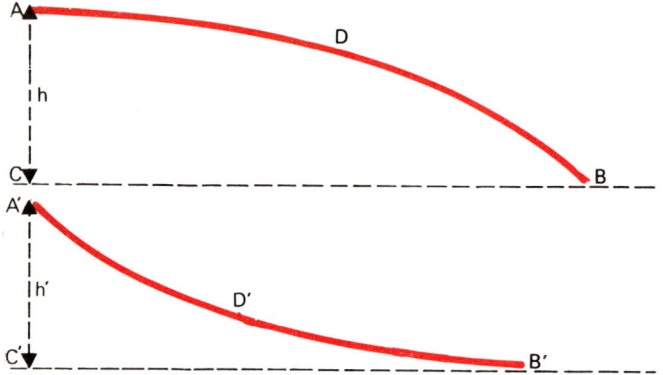

b. Suppose we have two stretches of track of equal length, and we make them into two slopes *ADB* and *A'D'B'*.

If we time model cars over these two slopes, which could be the fastest?

Or could we let the two cars go at the same time and see which reached the finishing line first?

c. In both *a* and *b* we are concerned with the time taken to run down a slope. This depends upon how quickly a car 'gets up' speed. Maybe the speeds at *B* and *B'* are the same, but the time taken depends upon the acceleration as well as the final speed. Ask the children about the speeds of the cars when they get to *B* and *B'*. Is one going faster than the other, if so, which one? Or, do they have the same speed? The answer they give will depend on their understanding of the concept of energy. At *A* and *A'* cars of the same weight have the same potential energy, so that if this is transformed into kinetic energy, the two kinetic energies must be the same, ie the speeds will be equal.

Maybe the speeds at *B* and *B'* are the same but the time taken depends upon the acceleration as well as the final speed. This can be appreciated if children have a knowledge of what the area under the curve denotes.

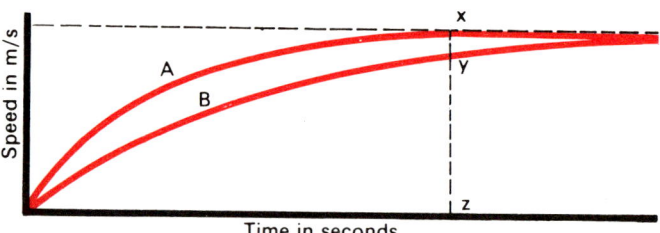

Take, for example, cars *A* and *B*. Both have the same top speed but *A* accelerates faster than *B*.

After *z* seconds *A* has reached a top speed of *x* m/s, while *B* has only reached *y* m/s. The distance covered by *A* is represented by the area *Oxz* and that covered by *B* by the area *Oyz*.

d. If we look at *a* and *b* again and ask about the speeds of the motors at *B* and *B'*, are they the same? How can we measure them? First, we need a 'measured mile' over which we can time the car; secondly, we need a timer. We could use a stop-watch or we could devise some electronic counting device (see section 6.5.2).

Another way of getting a comparative measure of the speeds is to run the same car successively down each slope, allow it to run into a cardboard box and measure how far the box is shifted each time. The distance shifted is proportional, in some degree, to the speed of impact. Therefore, if the box is moved the same distance each time, the speed of impact must be the same.

Note. If a plastics track is used, and then rolled up and kept like that until the next time it is used, it will be stiff and have taken on a semi-permanent set when it is unrolled. The track needs to be unrolled, weighted down so that it is straight and flat, and left overnight. Provided the room is warm, the kinks will have straightened out by the morning.

7.4.3 Switchback

If we freewheel down a hill, how far up the other side can we go before we come to rest?

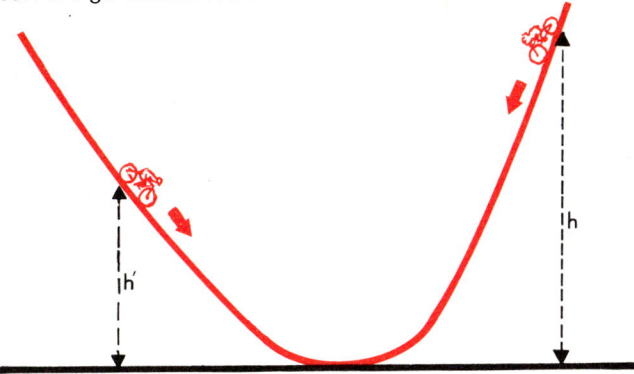

Why do we come to rest?

What forces slow us down? (gravitational, frictional, aerodynamic). Is it 'fair' to ignore wind resistance with a model car? What effect does wind resistance have? Could we make our model less streamlined and then try it again? Has h' altered? (Have we made sure that h is constant? If so, how?) Can some expression be obtained for the 'goodness' (efficiency) of a model? Perhaps it might be called the 'Index of Performance'.

For the same car, is h'/h a constant for different values of h? Measure h and h' and plot a graph.

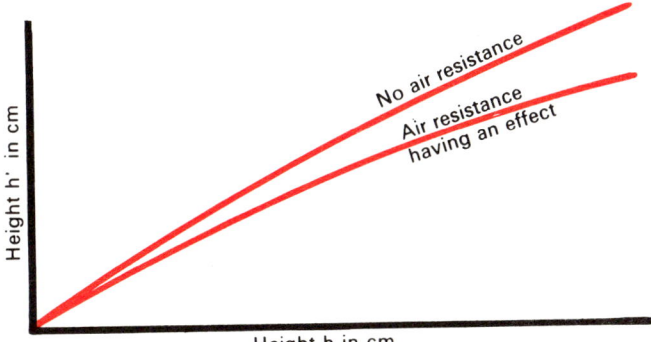

What kind of graph is it? What does this mean?

What is the effect of altering the angle of slope? Does h'/h alter? If it does alter, why is this?

7.4.4 Looping the loop

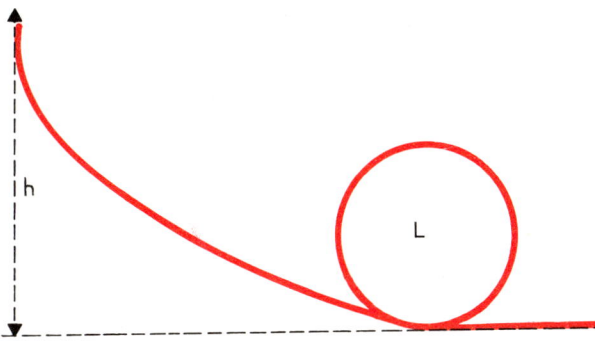

If the car is started from A, what is the largest diameter of L which still keeps the car on the track? If the height h is doubled, can the diameter of L be doubled?

7.4.5. Problems of weight

What effect does the putting of weights (washers, ball-bearings, pieces of lead) into a truck have on the speed it rolls down a slope?

If the brakes of a lorry completely fail, will the lorry go faster if it is loaded than if empty? Perhaps we can solve this problem by using toy trucks.

Once again we need to measure speeds.* In the absence of any speed-measuring instruments could we use the switchback and measure the vertical h', then

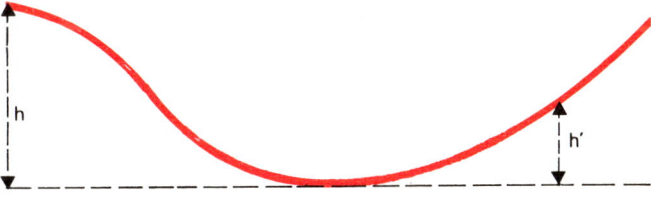

take this as being in some way dependent upon the speed of the truck? Is it fair to say that if two identical trucks rise to the same height then their speeds at the bottom of the dip are the same? (This assumes that frictional and aerodynamic losses are the same in both cases.) Is it fair to compare in this way two trucks having different weights?

---

*See section 6.5.2.

Another way of testing any ideas we may have is to have two tracks side by side and to run two trucks simultaneously down the slopes, one empty, the other loaded. To start both at the same time, hold a ruler across the tracks to keep the trucks from rolling, then remove the ruler by lifting it smartly. Change the weight from one truck to the other and repeat the experiment.

This will show if one truck has greater frictional and aerodynamic losses. To be fair, we ought to select two trucks which have identical losses at all speeds when empty.

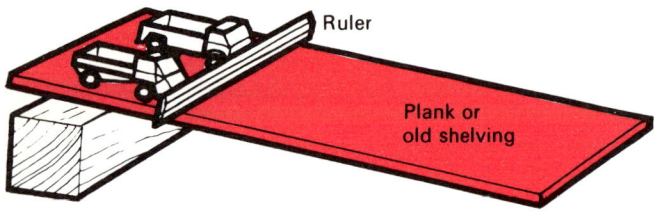

7.5 Electro Rockets

These cars are similar to the free-running models which are used on the Rockets track except that they are powered by a very small electric motor and an equally small rechargeable cell. The cell can be recharged from dry batteries and the length of the charging time can be controlled by means of an adjustable time-switch.

The dry batteries energise the cell, which in turn supplies energy to the motor: the nicad cell (nickel cadmium cell) acts as an energy store whose capacity can be varied.

7.5.1. Some investigations
a. Calibration of the time switch on the charger.

b. How long does the motor run on the track for different charging times? Is there any difference in the running time of the motor if the car is upside-down so that the motor runs freely without being under load?

c. How far does the car run for different times of charging?

d. What speed does the car attain? Use the timing device described in section 6.5.2.

e. What slope will the car climb?

f. Various ways of storing energy in toys could be compared, eg mechanical booster for Rockets, elastic motors, clockwork motors, inertia motors (flywheel motors), accumulators. (Make sure that you have a collection available.)

How is the energy stored?

The scale of storage required, eg could a full-size car be run on accumulators or an elastic motor?

How easy is it to store the energy?

Which method is most convenient?

What is the source of energy used to 'top up' the storage device?

g. The batteries in the charging unit are wired in series–parallel. The circuit for this could be examined and its advantages discussed.

7.5.2 Energy storage devices
There are three main ways of storing energy in a model other than those involving fuel or a source of electricity which cannot be recharged (eg a dry battery). These are:

Storing mechanical energy in a flywheel.

Storing the strain energy in a spring, etc.

Storing the energy resulting from chemical change in a rechargeable cell.*

Many toys provide examples of each of these methods. Pupils could be encouraged to bring to school examples of these toys. This would ensure that the teacher is kept in touch with developments in the toy trade.

*Details describing how to make and use a lead/acid accumulator are given in Change Stage 3.

8 Flying models

For thousands of years mankind dreamed of flying. Then, on November 21st, 1783, Pilatre de Rozier and the Marquis d'Arlandes became the first human balloonists. The balloon, made of paper by Joseph and Etienne Montgolfier, was filled with hot air. De Rozier and d'Arlandes were not the first balloonists; that honour must go to a cock, a duck and a sheep, which were the Montgolfiers' first passengers.

Within ten days of the hot-air balloonists' first trip, Professor J. A. C. Charles and N. Robert made the first ascent in a hydrogen balloon, but man's true conquest of the air had to wait for another hundred years. One branch of development led to the airship. The other branch, which seemed at first to be a pipe-dream, lead via Otto Lilienthal and his brother Gustav and the Wright brothers to the aeroplane.

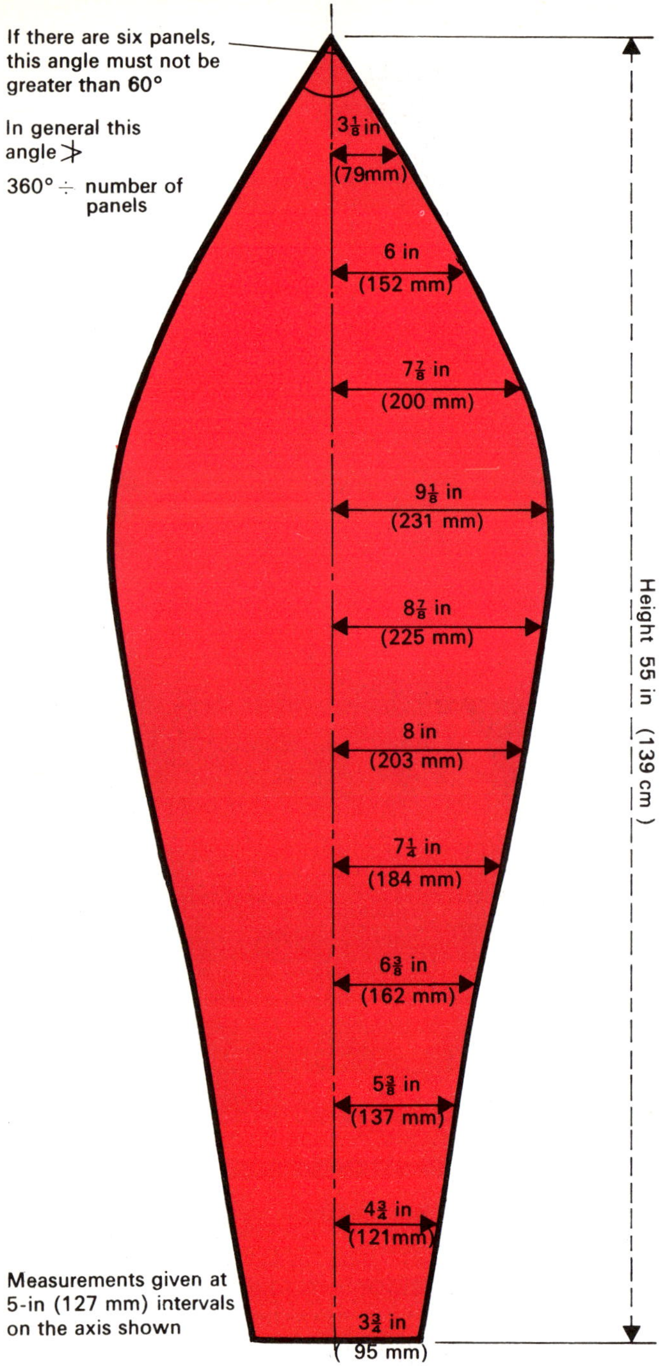

If there are six panels, this angle must not be greater than 60°

In general this angle ≥ 360° ÷ number of panels

3⅛ in (79mm)

6 in (152 mm)

7⅞ in (200 mm)

9⅛ in (231 mm)

8⅞ in (225 mm)

8 in (203 mm)

7¼ in (184 mm)

6⅜ in (162 mm)

5⅜ in (137 mm)

4¾ in (121mm)

3¾ in (95 mm)

Height 55 in (139 cm)

Measurements given at 5-in (127 mm) intervals on the axis shown

The same span of time separates the Concorde from the Spitfire as separated the Spitfire from the Wright brothers' plane.

The radio-controlled flying models* of today are far removed from the paper aeroplane or the cheap balsa wood glider, but all are subject to the same natural laws.

8.1 Hot-air balloons

8.1.1 Steps in the construction of a hot-air balloon

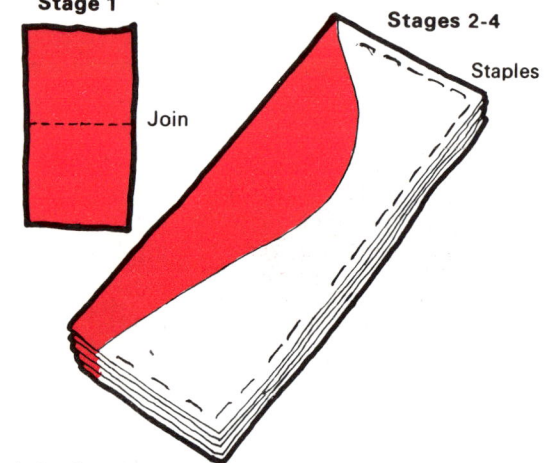
Stage 1 — Join
Stages 2-4 — Staples

1. Join the sheets of tissue paper to get six sheets 20 × 58 in [51 × 147 cm].

2. Fold the sheets lengthways and stack one on top of the other.

3. Staple together as shown above.

4. Mark out the shape with a felt-tip pen and then cut out with a sharp pair of scissors.

5. Lay one of the folded sections on a sheet of

The 1971 air-speed record for a radio-controlled model with a motor of 10cc was 213 mile/h! (What is that in km/h?).

newspaper. Run a *thin* continuous line of PVA glue*
about 1 cm in from the right-hand edge of the top fold.

6. Place another folded section on top of the first so that the two folded sheets are stuck together to form folds like a concertina.

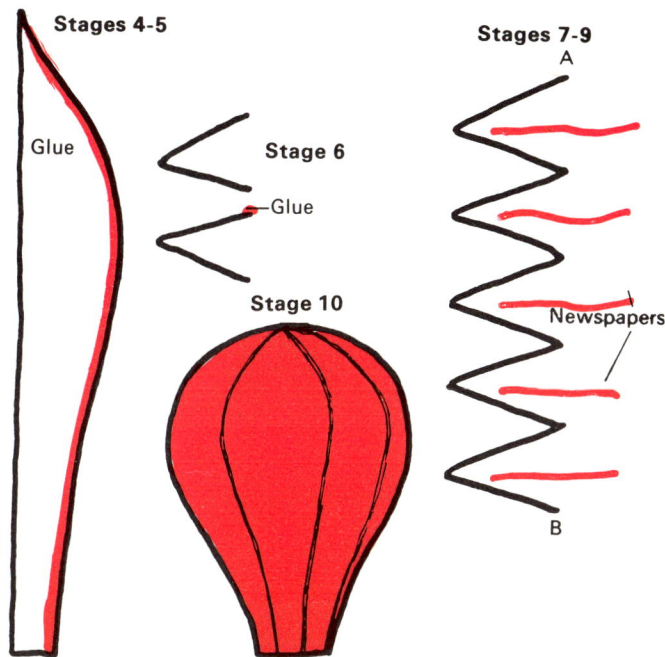

7. Carry on until all six sections are glued together.

8. Interleave the folds with newspaper to prevent the folds sticking together. Leave to dry.

9. Run a line of glue along the edge A and then complete the balloon shape by sticking together A and B. Leave to dry.

10. When the glue has dried, inflate the balloon using a hair dryer, vacuum cleaner, or hot-air blower.

Note. This is only to inflate the balloon to shape and dry it, not to fill it with hot air to make it lift.

---

*Any white glue will do, eg Evo-Stik Woodworking Adhesive. Do not use so much glue that it soaks through the tissue paper.

11. Making a heater:

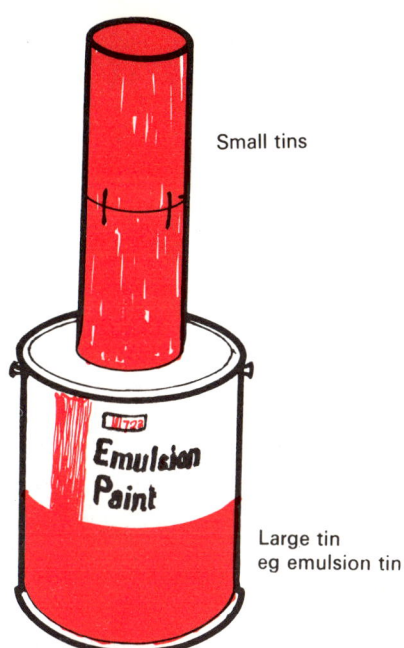

12. Light the methylated spirits and hold the balloon over the end of the two small tins.

This is safer than sending up a balloon with a burner hanging from it. A bunsen burner or a LPG picnic stove can also be used.

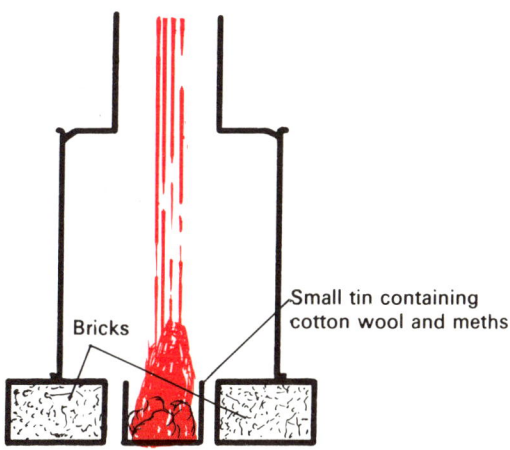

8.1.2 Flying hot-air balloons
Try filling the balloon in the classroom with hot air from a hot-air heater, hair dryer or Bunsen burner.

Take care that the balloon does not catch fire. Remember there must be some element of fire risk so take all precautions.

Only fly the balloon outside when there is a dead calm or a wind whose speed is not more than 3 mile/h [1·3 m/s].

Launching a balloon outside requires two people: one to hold the balloon and to pull the envelope open; the other to look after the heater and the neck of the balloon. Hold the balloon until the envelope fills and lift develops, then let it go.

It is strongly recommended that hot-air balloons be inflated by using a static heater, and that they are not sent up carrying any form of lighted material.

8.1.3 Working with a hot-air balloon
The hot-air balloon is a real winner, pupils being willing to spend a lot of their own time constructing one. It is a good starter for more conventional work on buoyancy, convection, expansion of gases, Charles's Law, transport, history of inventions, etc.

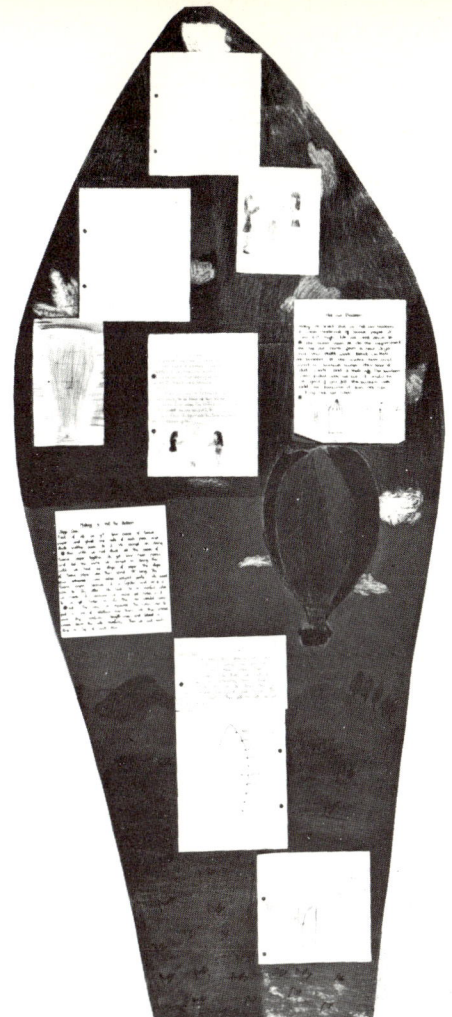

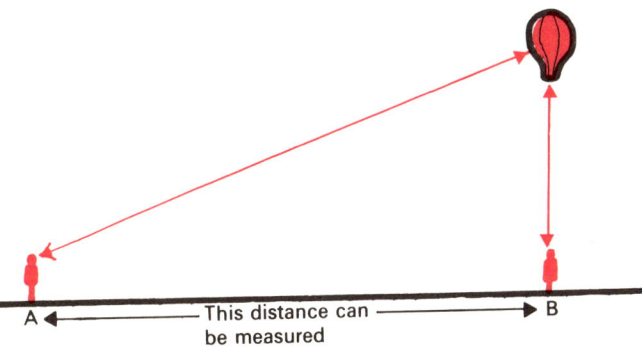

Note. Hot-air balloons work best on cold still days.

Other questions which could be asked:

How high does it go? How can the altitude be measured?

To find the height of a balloon, *A* uses a clinometer to measure the angle of elevation. *B* stands immediately below the balloon.

The distance between *A* and *B* is measured. A diagram is drawn to scale on graph paper. The problem resolves itself into constructing a triangle given one side and two angles.

11 year old boy.

How hot are the gases in the balloon?

What lift does it generate?

What is the theoretical lift? (This would be for more senior pupils.)

8.1.4 Development work
Make balloons of different sizes and shapes.

Could a hot-air balloon be used to take an aerial photograph?

Schools have used hydrogen balloons for this purpose, but inflating them is expensive. Hot-air balloons are cheaper to make and fly.

Is it possible to develop some system of tethering a balloon in a light wind?

8.2 Paper aeroplanes

Everybody seems to have made and flown paper aeroplanes, but few have set out to improve them by analysing their flying defects, and then making adjustments to improve their flying performance. In doing this, the experimenter acquires a knowledge of practical aerodynamics and learns how to experiment.

A recommended book for teachers is *How to Make and Fly Paper Aircraft* by Ralph S. Barnaby (John Murray, 1971). This book explains in non-technical language the principles of flight, and gives details of the construction of paper aircraft. It could form the basis of a number of work-cards.

What ideas, concepts and attitudes can be developed by working with paper flying models? Some of these might be:

An appreciation of air resistance and turbulence.

A knowledge of lift and how it is produced, leading to an appreciation of the Bernouilli effect.

A knowledge of centre of gravity and how the weight of a body appears to act through this point (under conditions of rest or constant velocity).

An appreciation of how the forces of lift, drag and gravity are in a state of balance (during a constant velocity flight). This leads on to stability and a knowledge of how a body can move about three axes set at right angles to one another.

The ability to identify variables and the appreciation that they need to be controlled when carrying out investigations.

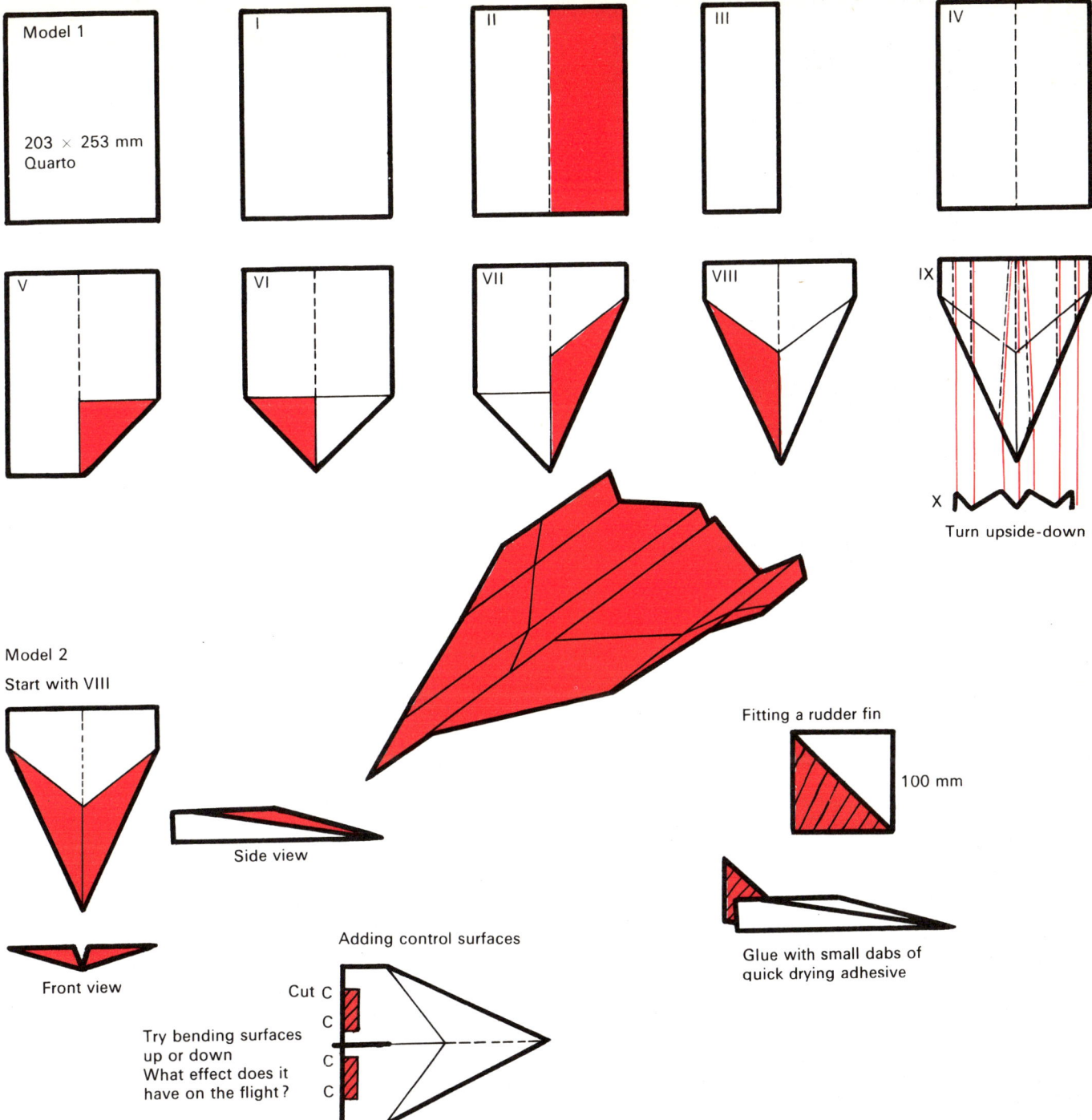

The sheer joy and interest of carrying out investigations overcoming difficulties and of producing something which is satisfying. Success breeds success, but an unsuccessful investigation, whatever the cause, only produces frustration.

8.2.1 Making paper aeroplanes

We can start with the simplest of flying models, the ubiquitous paper dart. This is easy to make but seldom does anyone consciously make an effort to produce a good flier or to consider why a model does not come up to expectations.

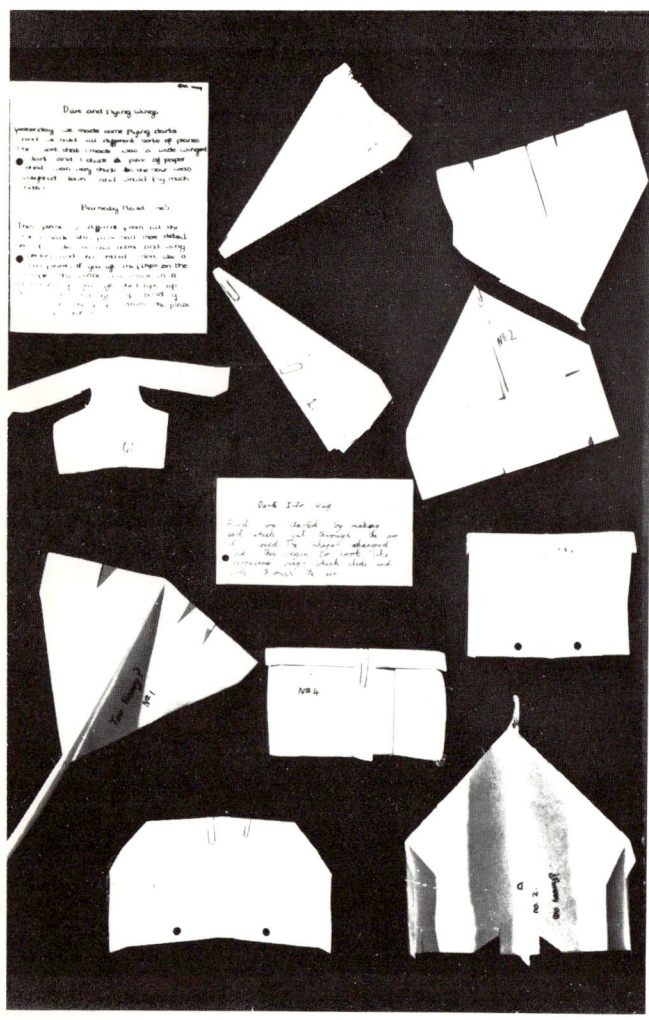

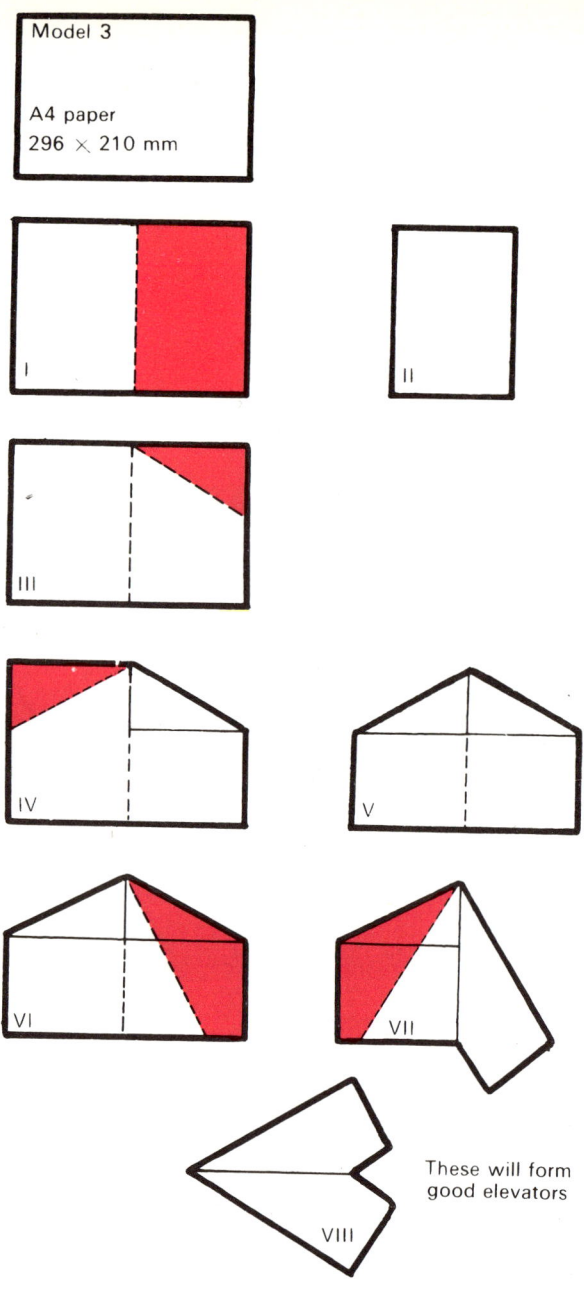

These will form good elevators

Gently throw the models very slightly downwards. Never throw them up. The throw should be a gentle push rather than a vigorous attempt to break a record.

8.2.2 Ideas to follow up

1. How is an aircraft made to climb and dive?

2. What is the point about which an aircraft will balance? Find it for each model and label it *X*.

What is the fraction $\frac{AX}{AD}$?

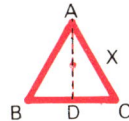

Is it approximately the same for the three models?

3. What forces act on a model as it glides?

4. What is the angle of glide?

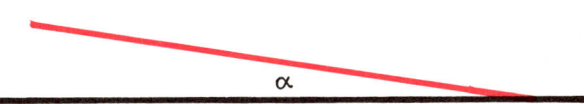

The models 1, 2, 3 glide quite well without having to add any extra weight. Any trimming is done by slightly bending the trailing edge (back edge) of the wing either up or down. This introduces extra forces.

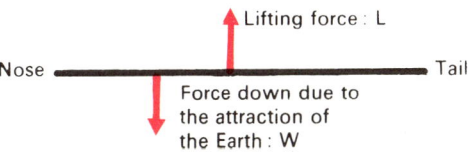

In this case, the weight is too far in front of the lifting force so the model dives to earth.

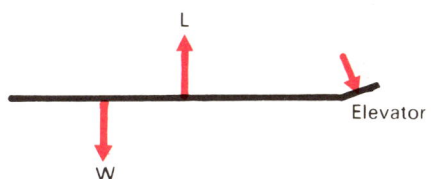

Now the control surface (elevator) is turned upwards and the air striking it produces a force, part of which acts downwards and helps to balance *W*.

8.3 Gliders

Gliders fascinate boys, but far too often they cannot fly them well and become discouraged. The snag is that a simple glider is quite a complicated affair, and to make it fly well is an exercise in sorting out variables; altering one factor at a time and noting the result; then going on and altering another factor.

To see what factors are involved, let us look at the simplest of models.

8.3.1 Three simple balsa models

Model 1
Such a model will fly if the Plasticine ballast is right, and this has to be determined by trial and error. It would be useful if the maker found out the point of balance of the plane. This is known as the *centre of gravity*, the point through which the weight acts.

Model 2
However, there are other factors at work. This time instead of glueing the main-plane directly on to the fuselage do the following:

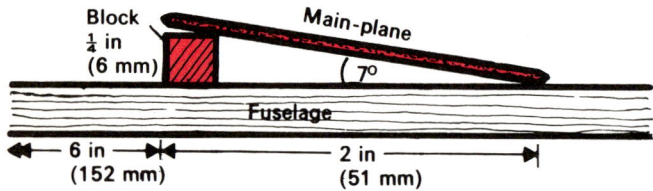

Glue a block ¼ in [6 mm] thick, 6 in [152 mm] back from the nose, and then stick the main-plane on top so that the leading (front) edge rests on the block and the trailing (back) edge on the fuselage.

This will mean that the main-plane will be pointing upwards at an angle of about 7° to the fuselage and the tail-plane.

Now try using different weights on the nose until the model glides well. Does Model 2 require the same amount of Plasticine as Model 1? Where is the centre of gravity of this model when it flies well?

Model 3
This is constructed as Model 1, only the *tail-plane* is stuck on differently.

This time a block 3/16 in [5 mm] thick is stuck on the end of the fuselage and then the tail-plane stuck in position as shown.

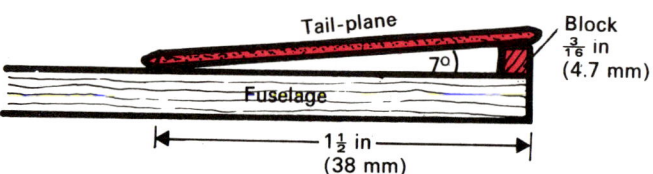

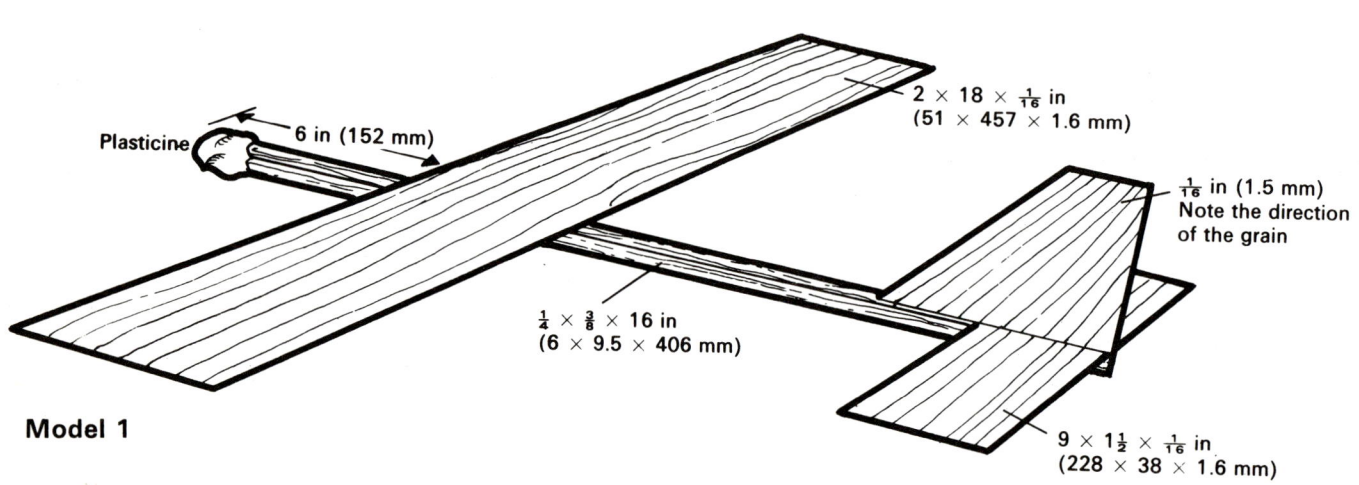

Model 1

This arrangement means that the tail-plane is pointing downwards at an angle of about 7°.

Now how much Plasticine is needed? Where is the centre of gravity?

This type of investigation could be pursued further with different angles between the planes and the fuselage.

So far, only the angles of the planes have been altered. Now go back to Model 1. Gum on to the main plane two strips of thin card each 3 in long by ¾ in wide [7 × 19 mm].

Bend the card downwards.

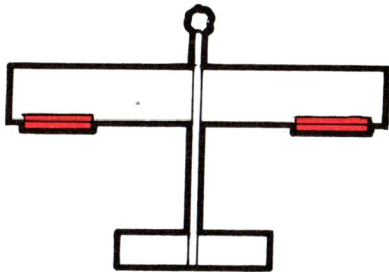

The card now forms a flap. Try retrimming the plane, and check the weight of Plasticine and position of the centre of gravity.

Try different angles of flap. Do you have to alter the weight of Plasticine?

Remove the strips of card and try a similar experiment with the tail-plane, only this time use strips and bend them *upwards*. Try altering the weights and the angle of the card (elevator).

For an aircraft that cannot be controlled, there is one more important feature that must be incorporated if the aircraft is to cope with gusts and turbulence: that is the two halves of the main-plane must form an extremely shallow V, called the dihedral. This makes the aircraft stable and enables it to right itself when thrown off balance. Like most other factors, there is an optimum. The angle depends on the type of aircraft. One of your models that is flying as well as you can get it could be modified to give the main-plane a dihedral.

Besides the dihedral, the position of the centre of gravity, the angle of the wings, the flaps and the elevators, there are other factors which influence the flying of the model. On the model itself, there are:

The section of the wings (we are using thin flat sections).

The length, width and shape of the wings.

The size and shape of the rudder-fin.

The distance between the main-plane and tail-plane.

The shape and size of the fuselage.

The total weight of the plane.

The conditions under which the model is flown are also important:

The strength and direction of the wind—always launch into the wind.

Whether there are upcurrents of air.

Turbulence and blustery conditions due to the wind blowing around obstacles.

With all these variables and a number of others that have not been mentioned, it is not surprising that flying model aircraft is a highly skilled pastime and that it is taken very seriously as a sport in some countries. World championships are held every year, and to become an expert requires a rare combination of skills and intelligence. However, the basic elements can be profitably investigated and they do provide an excellent example of tackling a task in a systematic fashion: changing the variables one at a time; identifying the effective variables; using controls; making measurements; being able to make predictions by using observations. These are all useful objectives.

The following instructions enable a 'chuck glider' to be made incorporating some of the important features. It is launched by holding the nose in the right hand with the forefinger behind the step then swinging the arm so that the plane is launched with its wings almost vertical.

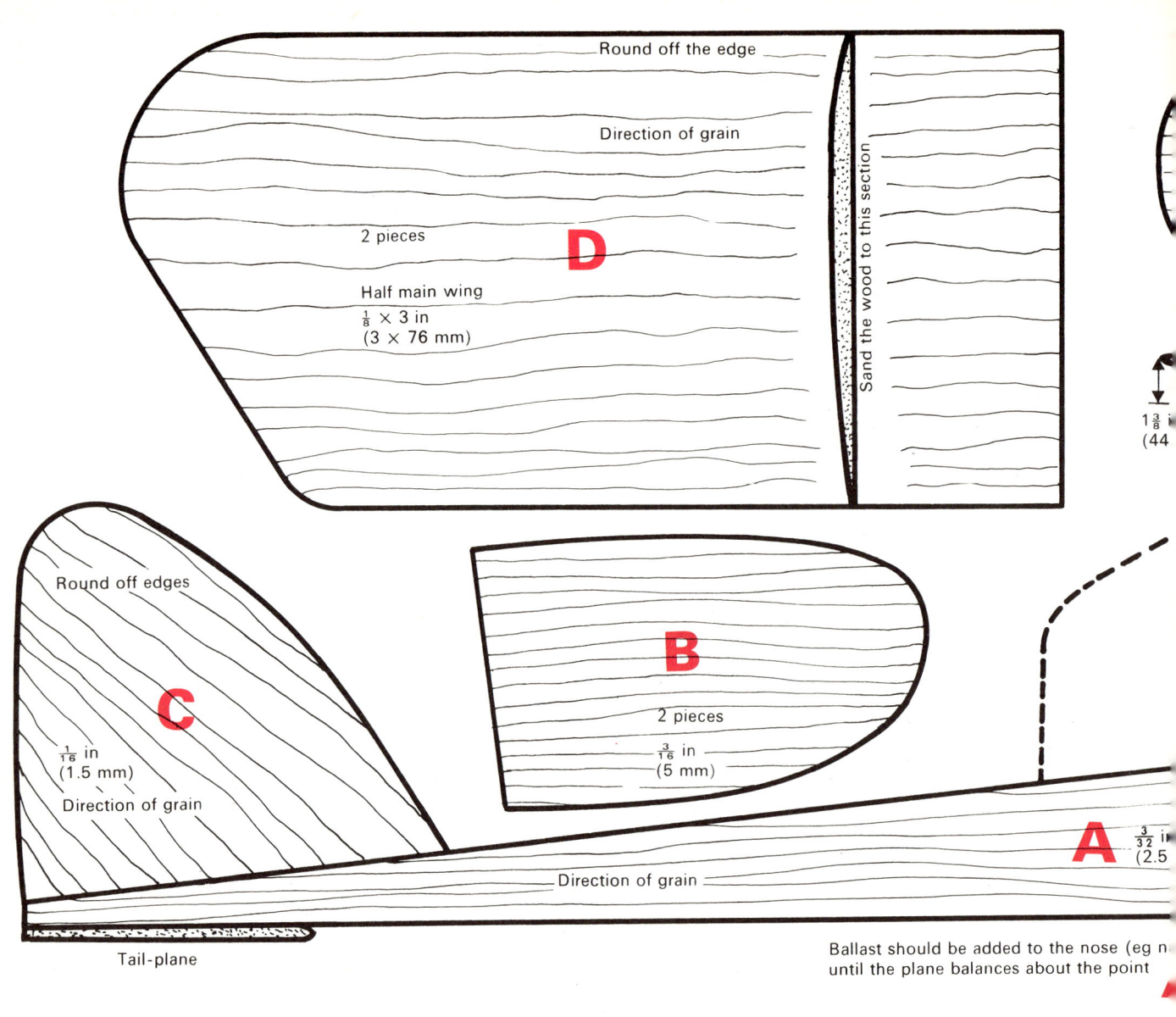

80

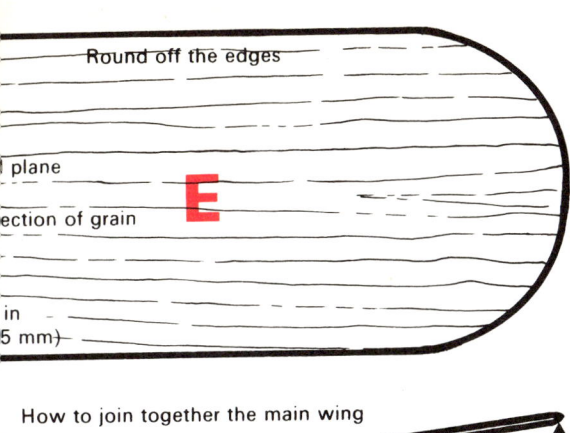
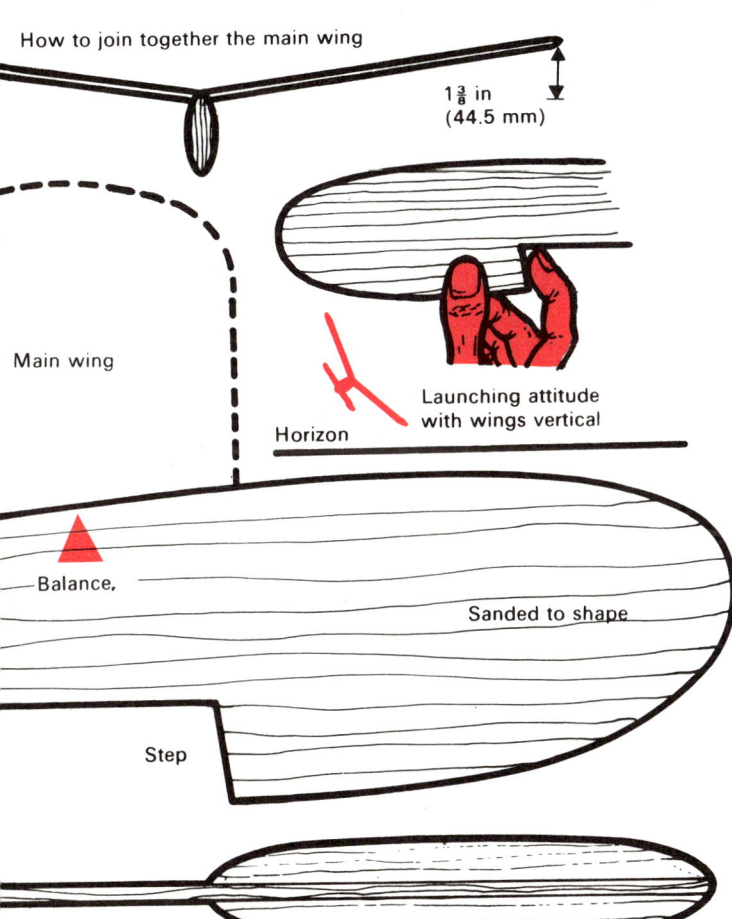

In this way, the glider will circle to the right and climb until it reaches maximum height when it will level off and begin gently turning *left*.

8.3.2 Solid balsa wood chuck glider
Materials required

One length of each of:

$3 \times \frac{1}{16}$ in [76 × 1.5mm] soft balsa wood.
$3 \times \frac{1}{8}$ in [76 × 3mm] soft balsa wood.
$2 \times \frac{3}{16}$ in [50 × 5mm] soft balsa wood.
$2 \times \frac{3}{32}$ in [50 × 2.5mm] hard balsa wood.

Fine sand-paper. Balsa cement. One-inch [25mm] nails.

Note. It may not be possible to obtain balsa wood in metric measurements.

Instructions
Follow these instructions step by step. Do not rush.

1. Cut out the parts *A–E* from balsa wood.

2. Using balsa cement, stick on the two pieces *B*, one each side of *A*. Use clothes pegs to hold the pieces in place and allow the cement to set.

3. Sand *C, D* and *E* to shape.

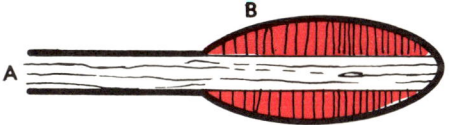

4. When *A* and *B* are stuck together, sand the forward edges until a streamline shape is produced.

5. Arrange the two halves of the main wing as below.

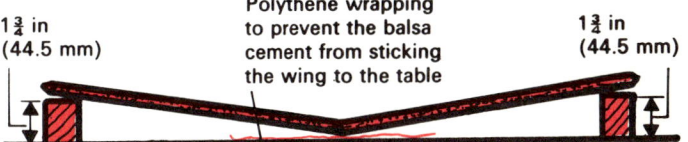

Sand the straight ends of the two halves so that they fit together, then apply the cement and push them together. The polythene wrapping prevents the cement from sticking to the table. Leave the cement to set for several hours.

6. Stick E on the rear of A and firmly secure it in position by two fillets.

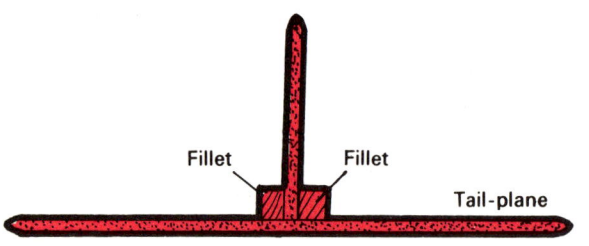

Use pins to hold the pieces in place until the cement has set. Make sure that the tail-plane is set at right angles to the fuselage A.

7. Fix the main-plane in position XX and use fillets to secure it in position. Use pins to hold it in place until the cement has set.

8. Allow the cement to set for twenty-four hours before testing the glider. Next check to see that the model balances at the point indicated. If it doesn't, push nails into the nose until balance is obtained. When the plane is trimmed the time has come to test it. *Do not throw the glider;* gently aim it at a point on the ground about 4 m away from you. The plane should glide gently to earth.

Possible faults:

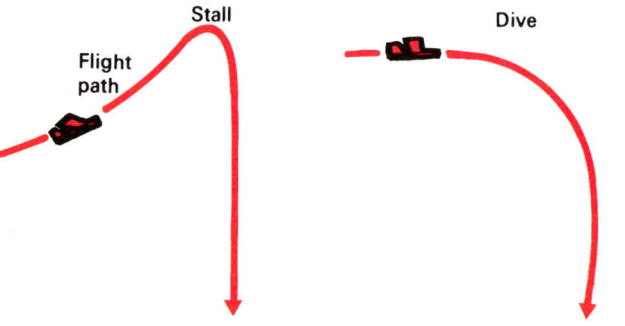

Stall: bend *down* the trailing (rear) edges of the tail-plane.
Dive: bend *up* the trailing edges of the tail-plane.

Now gently bend the rudder until the glider *gently* turns left. Only when the model is trimmed should you try giving it a 'strong arm' launch.

8.4 Flying models

Serious model-making, often embracing high levels of specialised knowledge, is fascinating but it is not for the beginner. Model and Allied Publications Ltd, 13/35 Bridge Street, Hemel Hempstead, Hertfordshire, publish over a hundred books; a catalogue is available from them. Besides reference books there are a number of monthly publications which provide plans and information for modellers, eg *Aero Modeller, Radio Modeller, Radio Control Models and Electronics.* It cannot be stressed too strongly that any beginner should start only with simple models. This may seem trite, but the present author has seen far too many beginners choose subjects which are intricate and suitable only for people with skill, experience and practical know-how. Far better start with something simple and make it successfully than try a complicated model which hardly works.

A beginner could do worse than start with an all-balsa glider. It is cheap and easy to make and the trimming to make it fly will provide experience for more complicated models. Once started, a useful book is *All About Model Aircraft* by Peter Chinn (MAP Ltd) which will act as a lead-in to powered model aircraft.

The subject has considerable potential in secondary schools, and quite large areas of the science, mathematics and craft syllabuses can be illustrated by, or based on, models. The modeller is concerned with:

The areas of wings of complex shapes.

Centres of gravity.

Forces in equilibrium.

Fuels and the energy released when they are burnt;

the composition of fuels containing compounds such as methanol, nitro-methane, nitro-ethane, amyl nitrite, amyl nitrate, nitro-benzene, paraffin and diethyl ether.

The working of a two-stroke diesel or a glowplug engine, using platinum wire as a catalyst, in the oxidation of methanol.

Paints, varnishes and dopes, and the effect on them of various solvents.

Glues, adhesives and cements.

Materials of many different types and their properties.

A modeller who designs his own models needs to be able to calculate and draw plans, and to have a working knowledge of structures and forces so that he knows whether a strut is in tension or compression.

Above all, a modeller needs patience and manipulative skill and common sense.

9 Objectives

Objectives are implicit in all the work described in this Unit. An explanation of Objectives and of what is meant by Stages is included at the end of this Unit. For a full treatment of the subject see *With objectives in mind*.

Besides these Objectives, which are of a general nature, teachers may devise others which may be more or less specific. For example, teachers may consider that knowledge of particular facts or modes of working is necessary. Certainly it is necessary to have in your mind some idea of what can be achieved if children tackle a particular investigation, but generally these Objectives need revising after the work has started.

For example, children working on cars and trucks may develop an interest in the production of petrol. This deviation from what the teacher had thought to be a logical progression need not be supressed, but a new set of objectives be formulated.

Because Objectives have been identified and recorded, it does not mean that a syllabus has been put together. Moreover, it does not mean that all Objectives listed at the end of this book must be covered like an examination syllabus. Objectives are intended to help teachers to see the relevance of work other than in terms of just why they are teaching a particular piece of work. The objectives we propose are not definitive ones but exemplify what can be erected. All we would hope is that teachers will make up their own Objectives, taking ours as examples, and that when their work has been completed, they will endeavour to find out to what the Objectives have been achieved.

Examples of Objectives appropriate to this Unit are given in sections 9.1–9.9.

9.1 Attitudes, interest and aesthetic awareness

These are the Objectives associated with curiosity, interest and keenness to find out things and they range from:

1.01 *Willingness to ask questions*, at an early age,

to:

3.12 *Willingness to extend methods used in science activities to other fields of experience*, by pupils who have *reached* a Stage 3 level of maturity.

In between these is a selection of objectives and these are implicit in all the Units of Science 5/13.

9.2 Observing, exploring and ordering observations

These Objectives tend to be more specific and relate to easily defined behavioural patterns. This being so it is also easier to pinpoint the Objectives in the text and to devise methods of testing how far they have been attained.

1.28 *Recognition of the action of force*, eg to cause motion and acceleration, bending, twisting, to oppose another force. Friction needs to be recognised as a force.

1.29 *Ability to distinguish regularity in events and motion*, eg the use of a pendulum for timing purposes.

2.26 *Ability to visualise objects from different angles and the shape of cross-sections.*

3.21 *Appreciation that classification criteria are arbitrary.*

3.22 *Ability to distinguish observations which are relevant to the solution of a problem from those which are not.*

3.23 *Ability to estimate the order of magnitude of physical quantities.*

Besides these examples teachers may formulate their own Objectives, for example:

Awareness of common effects of friction forces.

Awareness of ways in which objects fall to the ground.

Awareness of the typical shape of the path of a projectile.

Knowledge of some common physical properties of fluids (both gases and liquids), eg viscosity, streamline flow, turbulence.

9.3 Developing basic concepts and logical thinking

Generally, these Objectives are those associated with the development of concepts dealing with length, area, volume, weight, distance, time velocity and acceleration. It is important that these basic concepts are recognised by teachers and that some hierarchical system be erected as, for example, in the chapter on boats.

There are several very important Stage 3 Objectives associated with logical thinking which may be difficult to pinpoint but are essential for Stage 3 work. These are:

3.32 *Ability to separate, exclude or combine variables in approaching problems.*

3.33 *Ability to formulate hypotheses not dependent upon direct observation.*

3.34 *Ability to extend reasoning beyond the actual to the possible.*

3.35 *Ability to distinguish a logically sound proof from others less sound.*

9.4 Posing questions and devising experiments or investigations to answer them

All the Objectives listed are very pertinent to scientific investigations and can be roughly divided into those dealing with:

Variables.

Measurement.

Models.

Hypotheses.

9.5 Acquiring knowledge and learning skills

This section can be expanded to include the teacher's personal selection, but the list given could be described as being the minimum basic knowledge and skills. Not all of the Objectives are associated with work in this Unit; the following are explicitly dealt with:

1.56 *Awareness of sources of heat, light and electricity.*

1.57 *Knowledge that change can be produced in common substances.*

1.58 *Appreciation that ability to move or cause movement requires energy.*

2.52 *Familiarity with a wide range of forces and of ways in which they can be changed.*

2.53 *Knowledge of sources and simple properties of common forms of energy.*

2.55 Awareness of some discoveries and inventions by famous scientists.

2.58 Skill in devising and constructing simple apparatus.

2.59 Ability to select relevant information from books or other reference material.

3.51 Knowledge that chemical change results from interaction.

3.52 Knowledge that energy can be stored and converted in various ways.

3.53 Awareness of the universal nature of gravity.

3.55 Knowledge that properties of matter can be explained by reference to its particulate nature.

3.56 Knowledge of certain properties of heat, light, sound, electrical, mechanical and chemical energy.

9.6 Communicating

Nearly all of these objectives can be pinpointed because communication by words, pictures, writings, models, or mathematical representations, is essential in any form of education, and Stage 3 pupils should be able to use all modes. There are opportunities to use all methods of communication in this Unit (and be able to select an appropriate method to suit the information).

9.7 Appreciating patterns and relationships

The basic Objective is *1.81, Awareness of cause–effect relationships,* and an acceptance of this is fundamental to all our work in science.

You will notice that in Stages 2 and 3 the social implications of science are gradually introduced, for example:

2.85 Awareness of the changes in the physical environment brought about by man's activity; or

3.86 Appreciation of the social implications of man's changing use of materials, historic and contemporary.

One of the important areas of knowledge in all the common sciences (biology, chemistry, geology and physics) is that of energy:

1.56 Awareness of sources of heat, light and electricity.

1.58 Appreciation that ability to move or cause movement requires energy.

2.53 Knowledge of sources and simple properties of common forms of energy.

3.51 Knowledge that chemical change results from interaction.

3.52 Knowledge that energy can be stored and converted in various ways.

3.56 Knowledge of certain properties of heat, light, sound, electrical, mechanical and chemical energy.

3.84 Recognition that energy has many forms and is conserved when it is changed from one form to another.

Many of the successful toys utilise energy in some form.

9.8 Interpreting findings critically

2.93 Awareness that many factors need to be considered when choosing a material for a particular use.

2.94 Recognition of the role of chance in making measurements and experiments.

These objectives deal with measurements, accuracy, errors and flukes. How many times do you find pupils (even in the sixth form) measure a number of quantities to the nearest whole number and then give an average to two places of decimals? How many times do you find that a pupil relies on one measurement or determination?

Measurement and accuracy need not be a clinical exercise but could be introduced during an ordinary investigation. A similar exercise can arise in sixth-form chemistry, in which the determination of hypochlorides in solution can be a set exercise or it can arise as a *Which?* type test to find out the best buy of a number of bleaching solutions on sale.

9.9 The Unit and Objectives

The Unit contains suggestions for things children might do when exploring and investigating a particular subject area, these are easily recognisable.

It also contains Objectives since one aim of the Project is to encourage teachers to work 'with Objectives in mind'. These are less easy to recognise, and their function in the Unit is not so apparent as the children's activities. Here, we 'set the scene' for Objectives but we strongly recommend that teachers read the book *With objectives in mind* for fuller understanding.

Broadly speaking, Objectives are statements about what children might achieve from their work. They occur throughout the Unit, explicitly stated or implicitly there.

Recognising Objectives in the Unit

The 'Objectives for children learning science: guide lines to keep in mind', which you will find on pages 91–97, will help. It is reproduced from *With objectives in mind*.

There are two things to notice about the guide lines:

1. The Objectives have a particular arrangement based on their relationship to the Broad Aims* of the Project and to the stages of children's development which we have called Stages 1, 2 and 3.

2. The Objectives are numbered to indicate this relationship. The system of numbering is simple:

The *first* digit   indicates whether an Objective is at Stage 1, 2 or 3.

The *second* digit   indicates the Broad Aim under which the Objective is located.

The *third* digit   identifies the individual statement.

For example, the Objective *ability to construct models as a means of recording observations* is numbered 2.74. The number 2.74 has the following meaning:

2	*7*	*4*
This shows the stage in children's development to which the Objective chiefly applies—in this case Stage 2.	This shows the aim to which the Objective is expected to contribute—in this case .70 Communicating.	This shows the position (arbitrary) in the list of Stage 2 Objectives that contribute to *Communicating*.

The numbers are useful labels, allowing easy reference to a particular Objective without quoting it in full. They do not imply any order of priority among Objectives.

You will find a diagram of the Broad Aims and an explanation of the Stages on pages 91–97.

10 Apparatus and materials

This list does not include science apparatus.

Boats
2 m plastics guttering 5–6 in [127–152 mm].
Plastics pulleys.
Meccano parts 44 or 11a or 2×126; 18 b; 21 or 22 or 23; 2×59; 12.
Bolts, nuts, washers.
Toy boats.
Balsa wood 3×1 in [76×25 mm], 3×$\frac{3}{8}$ in [76×9 mm] (model shop).
Blocks of expanded polystyrene (builders' merchants).
Hot-wire polystyrene cutter (either laboratory-made or from decorator's shop).
Flat elastic, $\frac{1}{8}$ in [3 mm] upwards.
Sheet brass.
Glass beads.
Gear wheels, brass. ⎫
Piano wire—14 swg. ⎬ Model shop.
Electric motors. ⎭
Adhesives.
Monofilament. Nylon line (very fine).
Sawdust/aluminium powder.
Small nails/hooks.
Nuffield item no. 332 Fluid Flow Model.

Books
Keil Kraft Handbook (model shop).
Solarbo Book of Balsa Models.

Balls
A large collection of balls of different sizes and materials.
Plasticine.
Ball-bearings of different sizes.
H-channel curtain track.

Ballista—mangonel
Plasticine.
Dried peas.
Wood, 3×1 in [76×25 mm].
Nails.
Elastic bands.
Clothes pegs.
Pins.
Ice-lolly sticks.
Balsa wood.
Expanded polystyrene ceiling tiles.
Hot-wire cutter.
Adhesives.
Lead shot.
Long cardboard tube.

Camera
Old spectacle lenses.
A cheap camera which can be used by the members of the class; see section 5.7.

Photographic apparatus for developing and printing, eg enlarger, developing tank and dishes, bulk film loader, etc., see sections 5.5.1 and 5.5.2.
Matt black cardboard (or white cardboard painted with matt black paint—the small tins of paint used for painting models are just right).
Rubber bands.
Aluminium foil.
Black adhesive tape—passe-partout tape.
Ice-lolly stick.
Thick duplicating paper (for making blueprint paper).

(Not essential but of use to science and art departments: 'Fundamentals of Photography', a teaching kit by Kodak Ltd, 106H Education Service, Victoria Road, Ruislip, Middlesex.)

Books
Developing, Printing, Enlarging, Kodak Ltd.
Starting with Colour, Kodak Ltd. Very basic technical information.

Let's Take Colour Pictures Outdoors.
Close-ups in Colour.
Your Garden in Colour. } Useful for ideas and techniques.
Motor Sport in Colour.
Sailing in Colour.
Your Holiday in Colour.

De Mare, Eric, *Colour Photography,* Penguin Books. Gives an outline of the principles and historical development of colour photography.

De Mare, Eric, *Photography,* Penguin Books. A good general-purpose book on photography covering history, camera and how to use it and processing. Also contains a useful bibliography.

The British Journal Photographic Annual. Published yearly. Covers advances made in photography, materials and equipment during the year. Gives useful formulae and information; extensive bibliography.

Ilford Manual of Photography. Long regarded as the photographer's bible; has recently been revised.

Pippard, A. R., and MacDonnell, Kevin, *Home Photography,* Johnsons of Hendon. Very good indeed.

The Life Library of Photography, Time-Life Books, Time-Life International Ltd, Time & Life Buildings, New Bond Street, London W1E 8WE. A series of very useful books.

A useful book which is only obtainable from second-hand book shops is *The British Journal Photographic Almanac,* which was published yearly in crown octavo format until 1963. This book contained sections on chemicals, formulae and tables of information which are invaluable to experimenters. These books contained a mine of information and it is difficult to find any modern book presenting the same wide coverage.

Electrical toys
Some timing device, see sections 6.5.1 and 6.5.2.
Low-voltage pack, cheap electric model boat, electric model railway.
26 swg enamelled copper wire.
Small nails.
Ceramic ferrite magnets $50 \times 19 \times 6$ mm.
Dexion/Handy angle strips.

Books and magazines
Aero Modeller (monthly).
Practical Electronics (monthly).
Everyday Electronics (monthly).
Radio Modeller (monthly).
Radio Control Models and Electronics (monthly).
Wireless World (monthly).
Practical Radio (monthly).
Radio Constructor (monthly).
Warring, R. H., *Single Channel Radio Control,* MAP Ltd.
Warring, R. H., *Multi Channel Radio Control,* MAP Ltd.
Siposs, George, *Model Car Racing by Radio Control,* MAP Ltd.
Connolly, Phillip, and Smeed, Vic, *Radio Control, Model Boats,* MAP Ltd.

Trains and cars
Meccano—Parts 52, 72, 37, 19s, 59, 16; Gears 26, 27a, 27b, 28, 31, 32, 25, 27. Corgi Rockets set (with booster).

Timing device
An assortment of cars to run on this track.
910 Beach buggy can be loaded with weights.
Several lengths of Super Track (1963) for making parallel switchbacks.
Several lorries which can be loaded with weights and which will run on Super Track.
Corgi Electro Rockets.
Washers/ball-bearings.
Blocks of wood, G-clamps.
Plank of wood.

Flying models
One ream tissue paper, approximately 20×30 in [508×762 mm].
Aluminium cooking foil.
$\frac{1}{8}$ in [3 mm] square balsa cut from $\frac{1}{8} \times 3$ in [3×76 mm] sheet balsa (hard).

$\frac{1}{16} \times 3$ in [1·5 × 76 mm] hard balsa sheet.
$\frac{3}{32} \times 3$ in [2·5 × 76 mm] soft balsa sheet.
Balsa cement. PVA glue.

Books
Barnaby, Ralph S., *How to Make and Fly Paper Aircraft,* John Murray, 1971.

Keil Kraft Handbook.

Chinn, Peter, *All about Model Aircraft,* MAP Ltd.

Catalogue of books—Model and Allied Publications Ltd, 13–35 Bridge Street, Hemel Hempstead, Herts.

Fischertechnik
Fischertechnik is a system of interlocking materials, plastics and metal, for constructing models and various forms of apparatus. It can be used profitably by pupils of school age from infants to sixth-formers; it is flexible in its applications, and can be as simple or sophisticated as the situation demands. It came to our notice after we had written this book; had we known of it earlier we would have included in the text examples of its use.

Trials in eight Avon schools—infant, junior and a special schools—have shown that it can be a good educational tool, and a stimulus to communication and to creativity, having considerable potential in helping children to understand some topics in science and mathematics. It is made in West Germany and marketed in this country by Artur Fischer (UK) Ltd, 25 Newtown Road, Marlow, Bucks SL7 1JY.

Surplus Buying Agency
This is run by a consortium of local education authorities: Cumberland, Leicester, Northamptonshire, Nottingham, Sheffield, Southampton and Stoke on Trent.

It buys and sells at a very reasonable price items of use in a science laboratory.

Lists are issued.

Written inquiries to: A. W. Surguy, Manager, Surplus Buying Agency, Building A1, University Park, Nottingham NG7 2RD.

Objectives for children learning science
Guide lines to keep in mind

Broad Aims

- .00 .10 Developing interests, attitudes and aesthetic awareness
- .20 Observing, exploring and ordering observations
- .30 Developing basic concepts and logical thinking
- .40 Posing questions and devising experiments or investigations to answer them
- .50 .60 Acquiring knowledge and learning skills
- .70 Communicating
- .80 Appreciating patterns and relationships
- .90 Interpreting findings critically

Developing an enquiring mind and a scientific approach to problems

What we mean by Stage 1, Stage 2 and Stage 3

Attitudes, interests and aesthetic awareness

.00/.10

Stage 1
Transition from intuition to concrete operations. Infants generally.

The characteristics of thought among infant children differ in important respects from those of children over the age of about seven years. Infant thought has been described as 'intuitive' by Piaget; it is closely associated with physical action and is dominated by immediate observation. Generally, the infant is not able to think about or imagine the consequences of an action unless he has actually carried it out, nor is he yet likely to draw logical conclusions from his experiences. At this early stage the objectives are those concerned with active exploration of the immediate environment and the development of ability to discuss and communicate effectively: they relate to the kind of activities that are appropriate to these very young children, and which form an introduction to ways of exploring and of ordering observations.

1.01 Willingness to ask questions
1.02 Willingness to handle both living and non-living material.
1.03 Sensitivity to the need for giving proper care to living things.
1.04 Enjoyment in using all the senses for exploring and discriminating.
1.05 Willingness to collect material for observation or investigation.

Concrete operations. Early stage.

In this Stage, children are developing the ability to manipulate things mentally. At first this ability is limited to objects and materials that can be manipulated concretely, and even then only in a restricted way. The objectives here are concerned with developing these mental operations through exploration of concrete objects and materials—that is to say, objects and materials which, as physical things, have meaning for the child. Since older children, and even adults prefer an introduction to new ideas and problems through concrete example and physical exploration, these objectives are suitable for all children, whatever their age, who are being introduced to certain science activities for the first time.

1.06 Desire to find out things for oneself.
1.07 Willing participation in group work.
1.08 Willing compliance with safety regulations in handling tools and equipment.
1.09 Appreciation of the need to learn the meaning of new words and to use them correctly.

Stage 2
Concrete operations. Later stage.

In this Stage, a continuation of what Piaget calls the stage of concrete operations, the mental manipulations are becoming more varied and powerful. The developing ability to handle variables—for example, in dealing with multiple classification—means that problems can be solved in more ordered and quantitative ways than was previously possible. The objectives begin to be more specific to the exploration of the scientific aspects of the environment rather than to general experience, as previously. These objectives are developments of those of Stage 1 and depend on them for a foundation. They are those thought of as being appropriate for all children who have progressed from Stage 1 and not merely for nine- to eleven-year-olds.

2.01 Willingness to co-operate with others in science activities.
2.02 Willingness to observe objectively.
2.03 Appreciation of the reasons for safety regulations.
2.04 Enjoyment in examining ambiguity in the use of words.
2.05 Interest in choosing suitable means of expressing results and observations.
2.06 Willingness to assume responsibility for the proper care of living things.
2.07 Willingness to examine critically the results of their own and others' work.
2.08 Preference for putting ideas to test before accepting or rejecting them.
2.09 Appreciation that approximate methods of comparison may be more appropriate than careful measurements.

Stage 3
Transition to stage of abstract thinking.

This is the Stage in which, for some children, the ability to think about abstractions is developing. When this development is complete their thought is capable of dealing with the possible and hypothetical, and is not tied to the concrete and to the here and now. It may take place between eleven and thirteen for some able children, for some children it may happen later, and for others it may never occur. The objectives of this stage are ones which involve development of ability to use hypothetical reasoning and to separate and combine variables in a systematic way. They are appropriate to those who have achieved most of the Stage 2 objectives and who now show signs of ability to manipulate mentally ideas and propositions.

3.01 Acceptance of responsibility for their own and others' safety in experiments.
3.02 Preference for using words correctly.
3.03 Commitment to the idea of physical cause and effect.
3.04 Recognition of the need to standardise measurements.
3.05 Willingness to examine evidence critically.
3.06 Willingness to consider beforehand the usefulness of the results from a possible experiment.
3.07 Preference for choosing the most appropriate means of expressing results or observations.
3.08 Recognition of the need to acquire new skills.
3.09 Willingness to consider the role of science in everyday life.

Attitudes, interests and aesthetic awareness

.00/.10

Observing, exploring and ordering observations

.20

1.21 Appreciation of the variety of living things and materials in the environment.
1.22 Awareness of changes which take place as time passes.
1.23 Recognition of common shapes—square, circle, triangle.
1.24 Recognition of regularity in patterns.
1.25 Ability to group things consistently according to chosen or given criteria.

1.11 Awareness that there are various ways of testing out ideas and making observations.
1.12 Interest in comparing and classifying living or non-living things.
1.13 Enjoyment in comparing measurements with estimates.
1.14 Awareness that there are various ways of expressing results and observations.
1.15 Willingness to wait and to keep records in order to observe change in things.
1.16 Enjoyment in exploring the variety of living things in the environment.
1.17 Interest in discussing and comparing the aesthetic qualities of materials.

1.26 Awareness of the structure and form of living things.
1.27 Awareness of change of living things and non-living materials.
1.28 Recognition of the action of force
1.29 Ability to group living and non-living things by observable attributes.
1.29a Ability to distinguish regularity in events and motion.

2.11 Enjoyment in developing methods for solving problems or testing ideas.
2.12 Appreciation of the part that aesthetic qualities of materials play in determining their use.
2.13 Interest in the way discoveries were made in the past.

2.21 Awareness of internal structure in living and non-living things.
2.22 Ability to construct and use keys for identification.
2.23 Recognition of similar and congruent shapes.
2.24 Awareness of symmetry in shapes and structures.
2.25 Ability to classify living things and non-living materials in different ways.
2.26 Ability to visualise objects from different angles and the shape of cross-sections.

3.11 Appreciation of the main principles in the care of living things.
3.12 Willingness to extend methods used in science activities to other fields of experience.

3.21 Appreciation that classification criteria are arbitrary.
3.22 Ability to distinguish observations which are relevant to the solution of a problem from those which are not.
3.23 Ability to estimate the order of magnitude of physical quantities.

	Developing basic concepts and logical thinking .30	**Posing questions and devising experiments or investigations to answer them** .40
Stage 1 **Transition from intuition to concrete operations. Infants generally.**	1.31 Awareness of the meaning of words which describe various types of quantity. 1.32 Appreciation that things which are different may have features in common.	1.41 Ability to find answers to simple problems by investigation. 1.42 Ability to make comparisons in terms of one property or variable.
Concrete operations. Early stage.	1.33 Ability to predict the effect of certain changes through observation of similar changes. 1.34 Formation of the notions of the horizontal and the vertical. 1.35 Development of concepts of conservation of length and substance. 1.36 Awareness of the meaning of speed and of its relation to distance covered.	1.43 Appreciation of the need for measurement. 1.44 Awareness that more than one variable may be involved in a particular change.
Stage 2 **Concrete operations. Later stage.**	2.31 Appreciation of measurement as division into regular parts and repeated comparison with a unit. 2.32 Appreciation that comparisons can be made indirectly by use of an intermediary. 2.33 Development of concepts of conservation of weight, area and volume. 2.34 Appreciation of weight as a downward force. 2.35 Understanding of the speed, time, distance relation.	2.41 Ability to frame questions likely to be answered through investigations. 2.42 Ability to investigate variables and to discover effective ones. 2.43 Appreciation of the need to control variables and use controls in investigations. 2.44 Ability to choose and use either arbitrary or standard units of measurement as appropriate. 2.45 Ability to select a suitable degree of approximation and work to it. 2.46 Ability to use representational models for investigating problems or relationships.
Stage 3 **Transition to stage of abstract thinking.**	3.31 Familiarity with relationships involving velocity, distance, time, acceleration. 3.32 Ability to separate, exclude or combine variables in approaching problems. 3.33 Ability to formulate hypotheses not dependent upon direct observation. 3.34 Ability to extend reasoning beyond the actual to the possible. 3.35 Ability to distinguish a logically sound proof from others less sound.	3.41 Attempting to identify the essential steps in approaching a problem scientifically. 3.42 Ability to design experiments with effective controls for testing hypotheses. 3.43 Ability to visualise a hypothetical situation as a useful simplification of actual observations. 3.44 Ability to construct scale models for investigation and to appreciate implications of changing the scale.

Acquiring knowledge and learning skills

.50/.60

1.51 Ability to discriminate between different materials.
1.52 Awareness of the characteristics of living things.
1.53 Awareness of properties which materials can have.
1.54 Ability to use displayed reference material for identifying living and non-living things.

1.55 Familiarity with sources of sound.
1.56 Awareness of sources of heat, light and electricity.
1.57 Knowledge that change can be produced in common substances.
1.58 Appreciation that ability to move or cause movement requires energy.
1.59 Knowledge of differences in properties between and within common groups of materials.

1.61 Appreciation of man's use of other living things and their products.
1.62 Awareness that man's way of life has changed through the ages.
1.63 Skill in manipulating tools and materials.
1.64 Development of techniques for handling living things correctly.
1.65 Ability to use books for supplementing ideas or information.

2.51 Knowledge of conditions which promote changes in living things and non-living materials.
2.52 Familiarity with a wide range of forces and of ways in which they can be changed.
2.53 Knowledge of sources and simple properties of common forms of energy.
2.54 Knowledge of the origins of common materials.
2.55 Awareness of some discoveries and inventions by famous scientists.
2.56 Knowledge of ways to investigate and measure properties of living things and non-living materials.
2.57 Awareness of changes in the design of measuring instruments and tools during man's history.
2.58 Skill in devising and constructing simple apparatus.
2.59 Ability to select relevant information from books or other reference material.

3.51 Knowledge that chemical change results from interaction.
3.52 Knowledge that energy can be stored and converted in various ways.
3.53 Awareness of the universal nature of gravity.
3.54 Knowledge of the main constituents and variations in the composition of soil and of the earth.
3.55 Knowledge that properties of matter can be explained by reference to its particulate nature.
3.56 Knowledge of certain properties of heat, light, sound, electrical, mechanical and chemical energy.
3.57 Knowledge of a wide range of living organisms.
3.58 Development of the concept of an internal environment.
3.59 Knowledge of the nature and variations in basic life processes.

3.61 Appreciation of levels of organisation in living things.
3.62 Appreciation of the significance of the work and ideas of some famous scientists.
3.63 Ability to apply relevant knowledge without help of contextual cues.
3.64 Ability to use scientific equipment and instruments for extending the range of human senses.

	Communicating	**Appreciating patterns and relationships**
	.70	.80
Stage 1 **Transition from intuition to concrete operations.** **Infants generally.**	1.71 Ability to use new words appropriately. 1.72 Ability to record events in their sequences. 1.73 Ability to discuss and record impressions of living and non-living things in the environment. 1.74 Ability to use representational symbols for recording information on charts or block graphs.	1.81 Awareness of cause-effect relationships.
Concrete operations. Early stage.	1.75 Ability to tabulate information and use tables. 1.76 Familiarity with names of living things and non-living materials. 1.77 Ability to record impressions by making models, painting or drawing.	1.82 Development of a concept of environment. 1.83 Formation of a broad idea of variation in living things. 1.84 Awareness of seasonal changes in living things. 1.85 Awareness of differences in physical conditions between different parts of the Earth.
Stage 2 **Concrete operations.** **Later stage.**	2.71 Ability to use non-representational symbols in plans, charts, etc. 2.72 Ability to interpret observations in terms of trends and rates of change. 2.73 Ability to use histograms and other simple graphical forms for communicating data. 2.74 Ability to construct models as a means of recording observations.	2.81 Awareness of sequences of change in natural phenomena 2.82 Awareness of structure-function relationship in parts of living things. 2.83 Appreciation of interdependence among living things. 2.84 Awareness of the impact of man's activities on other living things. 2.85 Awareness of the changes in the physical environment brought about by man's activity. 2.86 Appreciation of the relationships of parts and wholes.
Stage 3 **Transition to stage of abstract thinking.**	3.71 Ability to select the graphical form most appropriate to the information being recorded. 3.72 Ability to use three-dimensional models or graphs for recording results. 3.73 Ability to deduce information from graphs: from gradient, area, intercept. 3.74 Ability to use analogies to explain scientific ideas and theories.	3.81 Recognition that the ratio of volume to surface area is significant. 3.82 Appreciation of the scale of the universe. 3.83 Understanding of the nature and significance of changes in living and non-living things. 3.84 Recognition that energy has many forms and is conserved when it is changed from one form to another. 3.85 Recognition of man's impact on living things—conservation, change, control. 3.86 Appreciation of the social implications of man's changing use of materials, historical and contemporary. 3.87 Appreciation of the social implications of research in science. 3.88 Appreciation of the role of science in the changing pattern of provision for human needs.

Interpreting findings critically

.90

1.91 Awareness that the apparent size, shape and relationships of things depend on the position of the observer.

1.92 Appreciation that properties of materials influence their use.

2.91 Appreciation of adaptation to environment.
2.92 Appreciation of how the form and structure of materials relate to their function and properties.
2.93 Awareness that many factors need to be considered when choosing a material for a particular use.
2.94 Recognition of the role of chance in making measurements and experiments.

3.91 Ability to draw from observations conclusions that are unbiased by preconception.
3.92 Willingness to accept factual evidence despite perceptual contradictions.
3.93 Awareness that the degree of accuracy of measurements has to be taken into account when results are interpreted.
3.94 Awareness that unstated assumptions can affect conclusions drawn from argument or experimental results.
3.95 Appreciation of the need to integrate findings into a simplifying generalisation.
3.96 Willingness to check that conclusions are consistent with further evidence.

These Stages we have chosen conform to modern ideas about children's learning. They conveniently describe for us the mental development of children between the ages of five and thirteen years, but it must be remembered that ALTHOUGH CHILDREN GO THROUGH THESE STAGES IN THE SAME ORDER THEY DO NOT GO THROUGH THEM AT THE SAME RATES.
SOME children achieve the later Stages at an early age.
SOME loiter in the early Stages for quite a time.
SOME never have the mental ability to develop to the later Stages.
ALL appear to be ragged in their movement from one Stage to another.
Our Stages, then, are not tied to chronological age, so in any one class of children there will be, almost certainly, some children at differing Stages of mental development.

Index

Adhesives, 21, 83
Aerodynamics, 22
   drag, 67
   paper aircraft studies, 74
Aircraft, 2, 22
   flying models, 82
   gliders, balsa models, 77
   paper models, 74
Apparatus, list, 88
Archimedes principle, 21
Atomic structures, ball bearing models, 40

Ball bearings
   in atomic structure models, 40
   in energy studies, 29
Ballista, 2, 30
Balloons
   hot-air, 70
   hydrogen, 74
Balls, 2
   bouncing, 24, 25
   rolling down slopes, 28
Balsa wood, in model gliders, 78
Batteries, 53
Bernouilli effect, 74
Bicycles, gears, 64
Blueprint materials, 37
Boats, 2
   in plastics guttering, 11
   pulley systems for, 12
   speed measurement, 12
   streamlining, 15
   towing force, 12
Bouncing, 25
Branching programme, fault finding, 58

Cameras, 2, 36, 49
   pinhole, 42
      working, 45
Cars, 60
   electrical racing models, 53
   gear ratios, 62
   models, energy studies, 2, 64
Centres of gravity, aircraft, 82

Clockwork motors, 21
Counters, electro-mechanical, 56
Creep, 19

Detergents, effects on boat's motion, 13
Developing films, 46
Diesel engines, 2, 19
Dislocations, ball-bearing photograms, 40
Distribution
   mangonel shots, 33
   measurements, 13
Dyes, 39

Elastic deformation, 18
Elastic motors, 17, 22
Electric motors, 19, 22
   making, 57
Electrical toys, 2, 51
'Electro-Rockets', energy studies, 68
Energy
   ball studies, 24
   and bouncing, 25
   lead shot, 34
   mangonel shots, 34
   model car studies, 64
   storage, 30, 68

Fault finding, 58
Flotation, 21
Friction
   model cars, 67
   rolling balls, 29
Fuels, energy release, 82

Gears, 60
   bicycles, 64
   cars, 62
   with elastic motors, 17
Gelatine/dichromate, 39
Graphs, three dimensional, 34
Gravitational forces, 67, 74
Group working, 4
Guttering, for boats, 11

Hills, model car studies, 65
Hydrodynamics, 22

Information sources, 10, 48
Integration, 10

Lead shot, heat energy, 34
Learning/teaching process, 7
Light-sensitive materials, 36, 46

Mangonel, 2, 30
   in energy studies, 31
   range, 31
   in statistics, 33
Measurements
   distribution of results, 13
      mangonel shots, 33
Meccano
   gear systems, 61
   pulley systems, 12
Models
   metal structure, 40
   in science teaching, 1
   see also specific models and toys
Moment of inertia, 29
Momentum, 25
Motors, 16
   see also Clockwork motors; Diesel engines; Elastic motors; Electric motors; Steam engines
Multivibrator, 54

Objectives, 84

Photo-silk-screen printing, 37
Photograms, 39
Photographic materials, 36
Photography, information sources, 48
   see also Cameras; Developing films; Printing films; Silk-screen printing
Piaget, formal operation stage, 3

Planning class work, 6
Polystyrene, boats, 15
Printing films, 47
Pulley systems, for pulling boats, 12
Pulling force, on boats, 12

Radio-controlled models, 59
Range, of mangonel, 31
Recording
   activities, with camera, 48
   observations, 8
Records, made by children, 8
Revolution counting, 19
Reynold's number, 12
Rolling balls down slopes, 28
Rubber, properties, 18
   see also Elastic motors

Safety, with electrical toys, 51
Shunting wagons, 52

Silk-screen printing, 37
Silver halides, 37
Sources of supply, 22, 59
Speed
   of model boats, 12
   of model cars, 65
Statistics,
   introducing, 33
   mangonel shots, 33
   measurements, 13
Steam engines, 2, 19
Streamlining
   boats, 15
   cars, 67
Submarines, 22

Telescopes, 46
Timers, electronic, 54
Towing, boats, 12
Toys, in science teaching, 1
   see also specific models and toys

Tracks,
   for ball bearings, 29
   for model cars, 67
Trains, 60
   electric, 53
Trajectories, 31
Turbulence, model aircraft studies, 79

Wakes, from boats, 14
Water
   motion of boat in, 12
   effect of additives, 13
Waves, from boats, 14
Weight, model *c*ar studies, 67
Work-cards, 8
   pin-hole camera, 42
Work-sheets, 8
   bouncing ball, 25

Illustration acknowledgements:

The publishers gratefully acknowledge the help given by the following in supplying photographs on the pages indicated:

G. Bosanko, 83
Daily Telegraph, 14 top right, 69
Education Development Center, 28
E. Keil & Co Limited, 20
Kodak Limited, 44
Bob Leitch, 72 right, 73 left
Don Radford, 3, 16, 191 32, 33
South West Picture Agency, 11, 12, 14 bottom left and right, 24, 30, 35
James Wright, 40, 41 top left and right, 42, 72 left, 73 right, 74, 76, 77

Line drawings by GWA Design Consultants Ltd.

Cover design by Peter Gauld